# Workshop on Graph-based Methods for Natural Language Processing 2012

# (TextGraphs-7)

**Held at the 50th Annual Meeting of the Association for Computational Linguistics (ACL 2012)**

## Jeju, Republic of Korea
## 13 July 2012

ISBN: 978-1-62748-344-5

**Printed from e-media with permission by:**

Curran Associates, Inc.
57 Morehouse Lane
Red Hook, NY 12571

**Some format issues inherent in the e-media version may also appear in this print version.**



Printed by Curran Associates, Inc. (2013)



Association for Computational Linguistics
209 N. Eighth Street
Stroudsburg, Pennsylvania 18360

Phone: 1-570-476-8006
Fax: 1-570-476-0860

acl@aclweb.org

**Additional copies of this publication are available from:**

Curran Associates, Inc.
57 Morehouse Lane
Red Hook, NY 12571 USA
Phone: 845-758-0400
Fax: 845-758-2634
Email: curran@proceedings.com
Web: www.proceedings.com

# Introduction

The TextGraphs is in its 7th edition. This workshops series brings together researchers interested in Graph Theory applied to Natural Language Processing and provides an environment for further integration of graph-based solutions into NLP tasks. The workshops encourage discussions about theoretical justifications from Graph Theory that explain empirical results obtained in the NLP community. As a consequence, a deeper understanding of new theories of graph-based algorithms is likely to help to create new approaches and widen the usage of graphs for NLP applications.

Recent years have shown an increased interest in integrating various aspects of the field of Graph Theory into Natural Language Processing. Many language phenomena can be naturally put into graph-based representations and in the last 5 years a significant number of NLP applications adopted efficient and elegant solutions from graph theoretical frameworks. These applications range from part-of-speech tagging, word sense disambiguation, ontology learning and parsing to information extraction, semantic role assignment, summarization and sentiment analysis to name but a few.

The emergence of new fields of research focusing on the social media such as Twitter and Facebook brought the graph-based methods even more into focus. In particular, graph-based algorithms are used to explore social network connections and propagation of information in those networks in addition to exploring the connections between the language entities. As a consequence, many new applications have been emerging such as rumor proliferation, e-reputation, multiple identity detection, language dynamics learning and future events prediction to name but a few. These new trends are reflected in the special theme for TextGraphs-7 "Understanding and Mining Social Media Using Graphs: Information Propagation in Blogs and Tweets".

The submissions to this year workshop were again of high quality and we had a competitive selection process. The accepted papers cover a broad range of topics from semantic similarity and word sense disambiguation to relation learning. Three papers cover the areas of the special theme, such as link analysis for twitter messages, social tagging, social network extraction.

The workshop series and the special theme are supported by the joint invited talk by Rada Mihalcea and Dragomir Radev.

The workshop organizers
Irina Matveeva, Gaël Dias and Ahmed Hassan

July 13, 2012
Jeju, Republic of Korea

**Organizers:**

Irina Matveeva, Dieselpoint Inc., USA
Gaël Dias, University of Caen Basse-Normandie, France
Ahmed Hassan, Miscrosoft Research, USA

**Program Committee:**

Chris Biemann, Darmstadt University of Technology, Germany
Guillaume Cleuziou, University of Orléans, France
Michael Gamon, Microsoft Research, USA
Andrew Goldberg, Microsoft Research, USA
Zornitsa Kozareva, ISI, University of Southern California, USA
Gina-Anne Levow, University of Washington, USA
Rada Mihalcea, University of North Texas, USA
Alessandro Moschitti, University of Trento, Italy
Animesh Mukherjee, ISI Foundation, Italy
Philippe Muller, Paul Sabatier University, France
Arzucan Özgür, Istanbul University, Turkey
Patrik Pantel, Microsoft Research, USA
Uwe Quasthoff, University of Leipzig, Germany
Dragomir Radev, University of Michigan, USA
Aitor Soroa, University of the Basque Country, Spain
Paul Tarau, University of North Texas, USA
Fabio Massimo Zanzotto, University of Rome, Italy
Torsten Zesch, Darmstadt University of Technology, Germany
Antoine Widlötocher, University of Caen Basse-Normandie, France

**Additional Reviewers:**

Veronica Perez-Rosas, University of North Texas, USA
Ravi Sinha, University of North Texas, USA

**Invited Speakers:**

Rada Mihalcea, University of North Texas, USA
Dragomir Radev, University of Michigan, USA

# Table of Contents

# Conference Program

**Friday July 13, 2012**

| | |
|---|---|
| 8:45 | Opening Remarks |
| 9:00 | Session 1 |
| 9:00 | Invited Talk by Rada Mihalcea and Dragomir Radev |
| 10:05 | *A New Parametric Estimation Method for Graph-based Clustering*<br>Javid Ebrahimi and Mohammad Saniee Abadeh |
| 10:30 | Coffee Break |
| 11:00 | Session 2 |
| 11:00 | *Extracting Signed Social Networks from Text*<br>Ahmed Hassan, Amjad Abu-Jbara and Dragomir Radev |
| 11:25 | *Using Link Analysis to Discover Interesting Messages Spread Across Twitter*<br>Min-Chul Yang, Jung-Tae Lee and Hae-Chang Rim |
| 11:50 | *Graph Based Similarity Measures for Synonym Extraction from Parsed Text*<br>Einat Minkov and William Cohen |
| 12:15 | Lunch Break |
| 14:00 | *Semantic Relatedness for Biomedical Word Sense Disambiguation*<br>Kiem-Hieu Nguyen and Cheol-Young Ock |
| 14:25 | *Identifying Untyped Relation Mentions in a Corpus given an Ontology*<br>Gabor Melli |
| 14:50 | *Cause-Effect Relation Learning*<br>Zornitsa Kozareva |
| 15:30 | Coffee Break |

**Friday July 13, 2012 (continued)**

16:00 Session 3

16:00 *Bringing the Associative Ability to Social Tag Recommendation*
Miao Fan, Yingnan Xiao and Qiang Zhou

16:25 Closing Session

# A New Parametric Estimation Method for Graph-based Clustering

**Javid Ebrahimi** and **Mohammad Saniee Abadeh**
Faculty of Electrical & Computer Engineering
Tarbiat Modares University
Tehran, Iran
{j.ebrahimi,saniee}@modares.ac.ir

**Abstract**

Relational clustering has received much attention from researchers in the last decade. In this paper we present a parametric method that employs a combination of both hard and soft clustering. Based on the corresponding Markov chain of an affinity matrix, we simulate a probability distribution on the states by defining a conditional probability for each subpopulation of states. This probabilistic model would enable us to use expectation maximization for parameter estimation. The effectiveness of the proposed approach is demonstrated on several real datasets against spectral clustering methods.

## 1 Introduction

Clustering methods based on pairwise similarity of data points have received much attention in machine learning circles and have been shown to be effective on a variety of tasks (Lin and Cohen, 2010; Macropol, et al., 2009; Ng, et al., 2001). Apart from pure relational data e.g. Biological networks (Jeong, et al., 2001), Social Networks (Kwak, et al., 2010), these methods can also be applied to none relational data them e.g. text (Ding, et al., 2001; Ng, et al., 2001), image (Shi and Malik 2000), where the edges indicate the affinity of the data points in the dataset.

Relational clustering has been addressed from different perspectives e.g. spectral learning (Ng, et al., 2001; Shi and Malik 2000), random walks (Meila and Shi 2000; Macropol, et al., 2009), trace maximization (Bui and Jones, 1993) and probabilistic models (Long, et al., 2007). Some works have proposed frameworks for a unified view of different approaches. In (Meila and Shi 2000) a random walk view of the spectral clustering algorithm in (Shi and Malik 2000) was presented. By selecting an appropriate kernel, kernel k-means and spectral clustering are also proved to be equivalent (Dhillon, et al., 2004). As shown in (von Luxburg, 2007) the basic idea behind most methods are somehow optimizing the normalized cut objective function.

We propose a new perspective on relational clustering where we use the corresponding Markov chain of a similarity graph to iteratively cluster the nodes. Starting from a random distribution of nodes in groups and given the transition probabilities of the Markov chain, we use expectation maximization (EM) to estimate the membership of nodes in each group to eventually find the best partitioning.

After a brief review of the literature in section 2, we present our clustering algorithm in detail (section 3) and report experiments and evaluation (section 4).

## 2 Background and Related Work

Due to the wealth of literature on the subject, it's a formidable task to give a thorough review of the research on relational clustering. Here we give a brief review of the papers that are more well-known or related to our work and refer the reader to (Chen and Ji 2010; Schaeffer 2007; von Luxburg, 2007) for more detailed surveys.

Graph clustering can be defined as finding $k$ disjoint clusters $C1,..Ck \subset V$ in a graph G = (V, E) where the vertices within each clusters are similar to each other and dissimilar to vertices in other clusters. Cut based measures, among others can be used to identify high quality clusters. Minimum cut of a graph is a *cut* (1) with the lowest value.

$$Cut = \sum_{l=1}^{c} \sum_{\substack{i \in C_l, \\ j \notin C_l}} w_{ij} \quad (1)$$

Here $c$ is the number of clusters and $C_l$ is the $l_{th}$ cluster. *Normalized cut* (2) is a better objective function that evades minimum cut's bias toward smaller clusters by incorporating total connection from each cluster to all nodes in the graph. In their seminal work Shi and Malik (2000) transformed the *normalized cut* to a constrained Rayleigh quotient and solved it by a standard eigenvalue system.

$$Normalized\_Cut = \sum_{l=1}^{c} \sum_{\substack{i \in C_l, \\ j \notin C_l, \\ u \in V}} \frac{w_{ij}}{w_{iu}} \quad (2)$$

Spectral clustering makes use of the spectrum of a graph: either the eigenvalues of its affinity matrix or its *Laplacian* matrix (Schaeffer 2007). For example in (Ng, et al., 2001) the $k$ largest eigenvectors of normalized graph *Laplacian* matrix is selected, the rows of the inverse of the resultant matrix are unit normalized and are finally clustered into $k$ clusters using k-means. Roughly speaking, spectral clustering embeds data points in a low-dimensional subspace extracted from the similarity matrix, however this dimension reduction may ensue poor results when the approximation is not good (Lin and Cohen 2010).

Meila and Shi (2000) showed that the corresponding stochastic matrix of an affinity matrix has the same eigenvectors as the normalized Laplacian matrix of the graph, thus spectral clustering can be interpreted as trying to find a partition of the graph such that the random walk stays long within the same cluster and seldom jumps between clusters (von Luxburg, 2007). The Markov clustering algorithm (MCL) (van Dongen 2000) is another algorithm that addresses graph clustering from a random walk point of view. MCL calculates powers of associated stochastic matrix of the network and strengthens the degree of connectivity of densely linked nodes while the sparse connections are weakened. Repeated random walk (RRW) (Macropol, et al., 2009) addresses MCL's sensitivity to large diameter clusters and uses random walk with restart method to calculate relevant score of connectivity between nodes in the network. Then, it repeatedly expands based on relevant scores to find clusters in which nodes are of high proximity. We should bear in mind that most random walk based algorithms have been designed primarily for biological networks where the number of clusters is unknown and some parameters e.g. desired granularity, minimum or maximum size of clusters might be needed for a meaningful interpretation of biological data. On the other hand, spectral clustering methods need to know the number of clusters beforehand but don't need tuning parameters and are more practical.

In this paper, we adopt an approach similar to probabilistic and partitional clustering in Euclidean space, where the algorithm starts from random guesses for some parameters and iteratively clusters the data and improves the guesses. In other words instead of embedding data points in the Eigen space or powering of the stochastic matrix, we're looking for a probabilistic model that solely employs the relation between data points.

# 3 Clustering Algorithm

## 3.1 Notation

Given a dataset $D = \{d^{(1)}, d^{(2)}, \dots d^{n}\}$, a similarity function $s(d^{(i)}, d^{(j)})$ is a function where $s(d^{(i)}, d^{(j)}) = s(d^{(j)}, d^{(i)})$ , $s \geq 0$ and $s = 0$ if $i = j$. An affinity matrix $A \in \mathcal{R}^{n \times n}$ is an undirected weighted graph defined by $A_{ij} = s(d^{(i)}, d^{(j)})$. after row-normalizing the affinity matrix, we find the stochastic matrix $P \in \mathcal{R}^{n \times n}$ of the corresponding Markov chain (MC) with states $\{X^{(1)}, X^{(2)}, \dots X^{n}\}$ where $\sum_{j=1}^{n} P_{ij} = 1$.

## 3.2 Hard-Soft Clustering

The basic idea behind Hard-Soft clustering (HSC) is to put nodes in clusters where within cluster transitions are more probable and between cluster transitions are minimal. *HSC* makes use of both hard and soft guesses for cluster membership. The method is parametric such that it estimates the hard guesses and uses the hard partition for soft (probabilistic) clustering of data. The mixture used to model hard guesses could be described by a mixture of multinomial model where the parameters (probabilities), are discretized {0, 1}. We start from random hard guesses and iteratively improve them by maximizing the likelihood using EM. Let $\{X^{(1)}, X^{(2)}, \dots X^{(n)}\}$ denote the states of the MC and given the number of clusters, what is the maximum likelihood of hard partitioning $H$ of nodes? Having $c$ as the number of clusters and $n$ as number of nodes $H$ is a $c \times n$ matrix that shows which node belongs to which cluster i.e. one in the corresponding element and zero otherwise. The likelihood function is as follows:

$$\ell(\theta) = \sum_{i=1}^{n} \log \sum_{z^{(i)}=1}^{c} Pr\left(X^{(i)} \middle| Z^{(i)}; \theta\right) Pr\left(Z^{(i)}; \phi\right) \quad (4)$$

In (4), $Z^{(i)} \sim Multinomial(\phi)$ is our latent random variable where the mixing coefficient $\phi_j$ gives $Pr(Z^{(i)} = j)$. For the soft clustering part of *HSC*, we define the prior distribution $Pr\left(X^{(i)} \middle| Z^{(i)} = j; \theta\right)$ as the probability of transitioning from $X^{(i)}$ to states marked by row vector $H_j$ $\left(\sum_{k=1}^{n} P_{ki} H_{jk}\right)$. This conditional prior distribution *simulates* a probability distribution on the states in the MC because $\Pr(X^{(i)})$ along with the joint distribution $\prod_{i=1}^{n} \Pr(X^{(i)})$ barely have any real world interpretation.

The E-step is computed using the Bayes rule:

$$W_j^{(i)} := Pr\left(Z^{(i)} = j \middle| X^{(i)}; \theta\right) = \frac{Pr\left(X^{(i)} \middle| Z^{(i)} = j; \theta\right) Pr\left(Z^{(i)} = j; \phi\right)}{\sum_{l=1}^{c} Pr\left(X^{(i)} | Z^{(i)} = l; \theta\right) Pr\left(Z^{(i)} = l; \phi\right)} \quad (5)$$

The M-step (6) is intractable because of the logarithm of the weighted sum of parameters.

$$\max_H L(H) = \sum_{i=1}^{n} \sum_{j=1}^{c} W_j^{(i)} \log \frac{\left(\sum_{k=1}^{n} P_{ki} H_{jk}\right) \phi_j}{W_j^{(i)}} \quad (6)$$

$$s.t \sum_{j=1}^{k} H_{jl} = 1$$

However since the weights are transition probabilities and $\sum_{k=1}^{n} P_{ki} = 1$, we can use weighted Jensen's inequality to find a lower bound for $L(H)$, get rid of logarithm of sums and convert it to sum of logarithms.

$$L(H) \geq \hat{L}(H) = \sum_{i=1}^{n} \sum_{j=1}^{c} W_j^{(i)} \left( \sum_{l=1}^{n} \log P_{il} H_{jl} + \log \phi_j - \log W_j^{(i)} \right)$$

The weighted Jensen's inequality $L(H) \geq \hat{L}(H)$ holds with equality if and only if for all the $H_{jl}$ with $P_{il} \neq 0$ are equal (Poonen 1999), which is not applicable to our case since taking the constraint into account, all nodes would have membership degrees to all clusters ( $H_{jl} = \frac{1}{c}$ ), therefore the inequality changes to a strict inequality ( note that we have relaxed the problem so that $H_{jl}$ can take fractional values that will eventually be discretized {0, 1}, for example setting one for the maximum and zero for the rest), Nevertheless maximizing the lower bound still improves previous estimates and is computationally more efficient than maximizing $L(H)$ itself which would require none linear optimization. Taking the constraint into account we use Lagrange multipliers to derive the parameters.

$$\mathcal{L}(H) = \sum_{i=1}^{n} \sum_{j=1}^{c} W_j^{(i)} \left( \sum_{l=1}^{n} \log P_{il} H_{jl} + \log \phi_j - \log W_j^{(i)} \right) - \lambda\left(\sum_{j=1}^{c} H_{jl} - 1\right)$$

$$\frac{\partial}{\partial H_{jk}} \mathcal{L}(H) = \sum_{i=1}^{n} W_j^{(i)} \frac{P_{il}}{H_{jl}} - \lambda = 0$$

$$H_{jl} = \frac{\sum_{i=1}^{n} W_j^{(i)} P_{il}}{\sum_{j=1}^{c} \sum_{i=1}^{n} W_j^{(i)} P_{il}} \quad (7)$$

To avoid bias toward larger clusters $H$ is further row-normalized. Similarly $\phi_j$ can be calculated:

$$\phi_j = \frac{1}{n} \sum_{i=1}^{n} W_j^{(i)} \quad (8)$$

**Algorithm**: HSC

**Input**: The stochastic matrix $P$ and the number of clusters $c$

Pick an initial $\phi$ and $H$.

repeat

E-step: $W_j^{(i)} = \frac{Pr\left(X^{(i)} | Z^{(i)} = j; H\right) \phi_j}{\sum_{l=1}^{c} Pr\left(X^{(i)} | Z^{(i)} = l; H\right) \phi_l}$

M-Step: $H_{jl} = \frac{\sum_{i=1}^{n} W_j^{(i)} P_{il}}{\sum_{j=1}^{c} \sum_{i=1}^{n} W_j^{(i)} P_{il}}$; $\phi_j = \frac{1}{n} \sum_{i=1}^{n} W_j^{(i)}$

Row-normalize and then discretize $H$.

until $H$ does not change

**Output**: the set of hard assignments $H$

# 4 Experiments

## 4.1 Datasets

We use datasets provided in (Lin and Cohen 2010). UbmcBlog (Kale, et.al, 2007) is a connected network dataset of 404 liberal and conservative political blogs mined from blog posts. AgBlog (Adamic and Glance 2005) is a connected network dataset of 1222 liberal and conservative political blogs mined from blog home pages. 20ng* are subsets of the 20 newsgroups text dataset. 20ngA contains 100 documents from *misc.forsale* and *soc.religion.christian*. 20ngB adds 100 documents to each category in 20ngA. 20ngC adds 200 from *talk.politics.guns* to 20ngB. 20ngD adds 200 from *rec.sport.baseball* to 20ngC. For the social network datasets (UbmcBlog, AgBlog), the affinity matrix is simply $w_{ij} = 1$ if blog $i$ has a link to $j$ or vice versa, otherwise $w_{ij} = 0$. For text data, the affinity matrix is simply the cosine similarity between feature vectors.

## 4.2 Evaluation

Since the ground truth for the datasets we have used is available, we evaluate the clustering results against the labels using three measures: *cluster purity* (Purity), *normalized mutual information* (NMI), and *Rand index* (RI). All three metrics are used to guarantee a more comprehensive evaluation of clustering results (for example, NMI takes into account cluster size distribution, which is disregarded by Purity). We refer the reader to (Manning, et. al 2008) for details regarding all these measures. In order to find the most likely result, each algorithm is run 100 times and the average in each criterion is reported.

## 4.3 Discussion

We compared the results of *HSC* against those of two state of the art spectral clustering methods Ncut (Shi and Malik 2000) and NJW (Ng, et al., 2001) and one recent method Pic (Lin and Cohen 2010) that uses truncated power iteration on a normalized affinity matrix, see Table 1. *HSC* scores highest on all text datasets, on all three evaluation metrics and just well on social network data. The main reason for the effectiveness of *HSC* is in its use of both local and global structure of the graph. While the conditional probability $Pr(X^{(i)}|Z^{(i)} = j; \theta)$ looks at the immediate transitions of state $X^{(i)}$, it uses $H_j$ for the target states which denotes a group of nodes that are being refined throughout the process. Using the stochastic matrix instead of embedding data points in the Eigen space or powering of the stochastic matrix may also be a contributing factor that demands future research.

As for convergence analysis of the algorithm, we resort to EM's convergence (Bormann 2004). The running complexity of spectral clustering methods is known to be of $O(|V||E|)$ (Chen and Ji 2010), *HSC* is in $O(|V|^2C^2I)$ where $|V|$ the number of nodes, $C$ is the number of clusters and $I$ is the number of iterations to converge. Figure 1 shows the average number of iterations that *HSC* took to converge.

| | | **Evaluation Method** | | |
|---|---|---|---|---|
| **DataSet (clusters)** | **Algorithm** | Purity | NMI | RI |
| UbmcBlog (2) | Ncut | 0.9530 | **0.7488** | 0.9104 |
| | NJW | 0.9530 | 0.7375 | 0.9104 |
| | Pic | 0.9480 | 0.7193 | 0.9014 |
| | HSC | **0.9532** | 0.7393 | **0.9108** |
| AgBlog (2) | Ncut | 0.5205 | 0.0060 | 0.5006 |
| | NJW | 0.5205 | 0.0006 | 0.5007 |
| | Pic | **0.9574** | **0.7465** | **0.9185** |
| | HSC | 0.9520 | 0.7243 | 0.9085 |
| 20ngA (2) | Ncut | 0.9600 | 0.7594 | 0.9232 |
| | NJW | 0.9600 | 0.7594 | 0.9232 |
| | Pic | 0.9600 | 0.7594 | 0.9232 |
| | HSC | **0.9640** | **0.7772** | **0.9306** |
| 20ngB (2) | Ncut | 0.5050 | 0.0096 | 0.5001 |
| | NJW | 0.5525 | 0.0842 | 0.5055 |
| | Pic | 0.8700 | 0.5230 | 0.7738 |
| | HSC | **0.9475** | **0.7097** | **0.9005** |
| 20ngC (3) | Ncut | 0.6183 | 0.3295 | 0.6750 |
| | NJW | 0.6317 | 0.3488 | 0.6860 |
| | Pic | 0.6933 | 0.4450 | 0.7363 |
| | HSC | **0.7082** | **0.4471** | **0.7448** |
| 20ngD (4) | Ncut | 0.4750 | 0.2385 | 0.6312 |
| | NJW | 0.5150 | 0.2959 | 0.6820 |
| | Pic | 0.5825 | 0.3133 | 0.7149 |
| | HSC | **0.6181** | **0.3795** | **0.7482** |
| Average | Ncut | 0.6719 | 0.3486 | 0.6900 |
| | NJW | 0.6887 | 0.3710 | 0.7013 |
| | Pic | 0.8352 | 0.5844 | 0.8280 |
| | HSC | **0.8571** | **0.6295** | **0.8572** |

Table : Clustering performance of HSC and three clustering algorithms on several datasets, for each dataset bold numbers are the highest in a column.

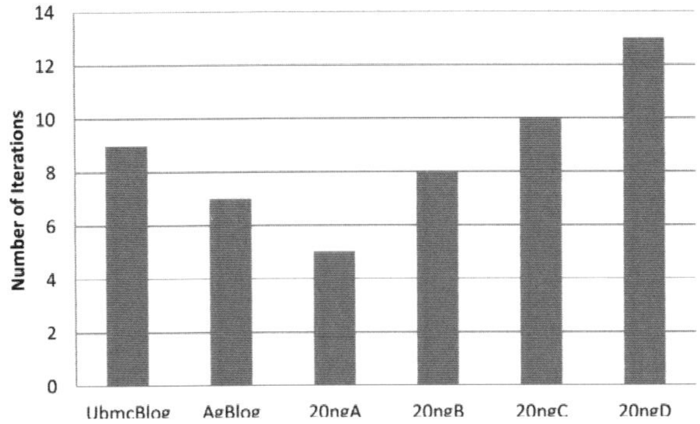


Figure 1: Average number of iterations to converge

## 5 Conclusion and Future Work

We propose a novel and simple clustering method, *HSC*, based on approximate estimation of the hard assignments of nodes to clusters. The hard grouping of the data is used to simulate a probability distribution on the corresponding Markov chain. It is easy to understand, implement and is parallelizable. Experiments on a number of different types of labeled datasets show that with a reasonable cost of time *HSC* is able to obtain high quality clusters, compared to three spectral clustering methods. One advantage of our method is its applicability to directed graphs that will be addressed in future works.

## References

A. Kale, A. Karandikar, P. Kolari, A. Java, T. Finin and A. Joshi. 2007. Modeling trust and influence in the blogosphere using link polarity. In proceedings of the International Conference on Weblogs and Social Media, ICWSM.

A. Ng, M. Jordan, and Y. Weiss. 2001. On spectral clustering: Analysis and an algorithm. In Dietterich, T., Becker, S., and Ghahramani, Z., editors, Advances in Neural Information Processing Systems, pages 849–856.

B. Long, Z. M. Zhang, and P. S. Yu. 2007. A probabilistic framework for relational clustering. In KDD '07: Proceedings of the 13th ACM SIGKDD international conference on Knowledge discovery and data mining, pages 470–479.

B. Poonen. 1999. Inequalities. Berkeley Math Circle.

C. D. Manning, P. Raghavan and H. Schu□tze. 2008. Introduction to Information Retrieval. Cambridge University Press.

C. H. Q. Ding, X. He, H. Zha, M. Gu and H. D. Simon. 2001. A min-max cut algorithm for graph partitioning and data clustering. In Proceedings of ICDM 2001, pages 107–114.

F. Lin and W. Cohen. 2010. Power iteration clustering. ICML.

H. Jeong, S. P. Mason, A. L. Barabasi and Z. N. Oltvai. 2001. Lethality and centrality in protein networks. Nature, 411(6833):41–42

H. Kwak, C. Lee, H. Park and S. Moon. 2010. What is twitter, a social network or a news media? In Proceedings of the 19th international conference on World Wide Web, WWW '10, pages 591–600.

I. Dhillon, Y. Guan, and B. Kulis. 2004. A unified view of kernel k-means, spectral clustering and graph cuts. Technical Report TR-04-25. UTCS.

J. Shi and J. Malik, 2000. Normalized cuts and image segmentation. IEEE Transactions on Pattern Analysis and Machine Intelligence, 22(8):888–905.

K. Macropol, T. Can and A. Singh. 2009. RRW: repeated random walks on genome-scale protein networks for local cluster discovery. BMC Bioinformatics, 10(1):283+.

L. A. Adamic and N. Glance. 2005. The political blogosphere and the 2004 U.S. election: divided they blog. In Proceedings of the 3rd international workshop on Link discovery, LinkKDD '05, pages 36–43.

M. Meila and J. Shi. 2000. Learning segmentation by random walks. In NIPS, pages 873–879.

S. Bormann. 2004. The expectation maximization algorithm: A short tutorial.

S. Schaeffer, 2007. Graph clustering. Computer Science Review, 1(1):27–64.

S. M. van Dongen, 2000. Graph Clustering by Flow Simulation. PhD thesis, University of Utrecht, The Netherlands.

T. N. Bui and C. Jones, 1993. A Heuristic for Reducing Fill-In in Sparse Matrix Factorization", in Proc. PPSC, pp.445-452.

U. von Luxburg, 2007. A tutorial on spectral clustering. Statistics and Computing, 17(4):395–416.

Z. Chen and H. Ji. 2010. Graph-based clustering for computational linguistics: A survey. In Proceedings of the 2010 Workshop on Graph-based Methods for Natural Language Processing, TextGraphs-5, pages 1–9, ACL.

# Extracting Signed Social Networks From Text

**Ahmed Hassan**
Microsoft Research
Redmond, WA, USA
hassanam@microsoft.com

**Amjad Abu-Jbara**
EECS Department
University of Michigan
Ann Arbor, MI, USA
amjbara@umich.edu

**Dragomir Radev**
EECS Department
University of Michigan
Ann Arbor, MI, USA
radev@umich.edu

## Abstract

Most of the research on social networks has almost exclusively focused on positive links between entities. There are much more insights that we may gain by generalizing social networks to the signed case where both positive and negative edges are considered. One of the reasons why signed social networks have received less attention that networks based on positive links only is the lack of an explicit notion of negative relations in most social network applications. However, most such applications have text embedded in the social network. Applying linguistic analysis techniques to this text enables us to identify both positive and negative interactions. In this work, we propose a new method to automatically construct a signed social network from text. The resulting networks have a polarity associated with every edge. Edge polarity is a means for indicating a positive or negative affinity between two individuals. We apply the proposed method to a larger amount of online discussion posts. Experiments show that the proposed method is capable of constructing networks from text with high accuracy. We also connect out analysis to social psychology theories of signed network, namely the structural balance theory.

## 1 Introduction

A great body of research work has focused on social network analysis. Social network analysis plays a huge role in understanding and improving social computing applications. Most of this research has almost exclusively focused on positive links between individuals (e.g. friends, fans, followers, etc.). However, if we carefully examine the relationships between individuals in online communities, we will find out that limiting links to positive interactions is a very simplistic assumption. It is true that people show positive attitude by labeling others as friends, and showing agreement, but they also show disagreement, and antagonism toward other members of the online community. Discussion forums are one example that makes it clear that considering both positive and negative interactions is essential for understanding the rich relationships that develop between individuals in online communities.

If considering both negative and positive interactions will provide much more insight toward understanding the social network, why did most of previous work only focus on positive interactions? We think that one of the main reasons behind this is the lack of a notion for explicitly labeling negative relations. For example, most social web applications allow people to mark others as friends, like them, follow them, etc. However, they do not allow people to explicitly label negative relations with others.

Previous work has built networks from discussions by linking people who reply to one another. Even though, the mere fact that $X$ replied to $Y$'s post does show an interaction, it does not tell us anything about the type of that interaction. In this case, the type of interaction is not readily available; however it may be mined from the text that underlies the social network. Hence, if we examine the text exchanged between individuals, we may be able to come up with conclusions about, not only the existence of an interaction, but also its type.

In this work, we apply Natural Language Processing techniques to text correspondences exchanged between individuals to identify the underlying signed social structure in online communities. We present and compare several algorithms for identifying user attitude and for automatically constructing a signed social network representation. We apply the proposed methods to a large set of discussion posts. We evaluate the performance using a manually labeled dataset.

The input to our algorithm is a set of text correspondences exchanged between users (e.g. posts or comments). The output is a *signed network* where edges signify the existence of an interaction between two users. The resulting network has polarity associated with every edge. Edge polarity is a means for indicating a positive or negative affinity between two individuals.

The proposed method was applied to a very large dataset of online discussions. To evaluate our automated procedure, we asked human annotators to examine text correspondences exchanged between individuals and judge whether their interaction is positive or negative. We compared the edge signs that had been automatically identified to edges manually created by human annotators.

We also connected our analysis to social psychology theories, namely the Structural Balance Theory (Heider, 1946). The balance theory has been shown to hold both theoretically (Heider, 1946) and empirically (Leskovec et al., 2010b) for a variety of social community settings. Showing that it also holds for our *automatically* constructed network further validates our results.

The rest of the paper is structured as follows. In section 2, we review some of the related prior work on mining sentiment from text, mining online discussions, extracting social networks from text, and analyzing signed social networks. We define our problem and explain our approach in Section 3. Section 4 describes our dataset. Results and discussion are presented in Section 5. We present a possible application for the proposed approach in Section 6. We conclude in Section 7.

## 2 Related Work

In this section, we survey several lines of research that are related to our work.

### 2.1 Mining Sentiment from Text

Our general goal of mining attitude from one individual toward another makes our work related to a huge body of work on sentiment analysis. One such line of research is the well-studied problem of identifying the of individual words. In previous work, Hatzivassiloglou and McKeown (1997) proposed a method to identify the polarity of adjectives based on conjunctions linking them in a large corpus. Turney and Littman (2003) used statistical measures to find the association between a given word and a set of positive/negative seed words. Takamura et al. (2005) used the spin model to extract word semantic orientation. Finally, Hassan and Radev (2010) use a random walk model defined over a word relatedness graph to classify words as either positive or negative.

Subjectivity analysis is yet another research line that is closely related to our general goal of mining attitude. The objective of subjectivity analysis is to identify text that presents opinion as opposed to objective text that presents factual information (Wiebe, 2000). Prior work on subjectivity analysis mainly consists of two main categories: subjectivity of a phrase or word is analyzed regardless of the context (Wiebe, 2000; Hatzivassiloglou and Wiebe, 2000; Banea et al., 2008), or within its context (Riloff and Wiebe, 2003; Yu and Hatzivassiloglou, 2003; Nasukawa and Yi, 2003; Popescu and Etzioni, 2005). Hassan et al. (2010) presents a method for identifying sentences that display an attitude from the text writer toward the text recipient. Our work is different from subjectivity analysis because we are not only interested in discriminating between opinions and facts. Rather, we are interested in identifying the polarity of interactions between individuals. Our method is not restricted to phrases or words, rather it generalizes this to identifying the polarity of an interaction between two individuals based on several posts they exchange.

### 2.2 Mining Online Discussions

Our use of discussion threads as a source of data connects us to some previous work on mining online discussions. Lin et al. (2009) proposed a sparse coding-based model that simultaneously models semantics and structure of threaded discussions. Huang et al. (2007) learn SVM classifiers from data to extract (thread-title, reply) pairs. Their objective was to build a chatbot for a certain domain using knowledge from online discussion forums. Shen et al. (2006) proposed three clustering methods for exploiting the temporal information in discussion streams, as well as an algorithm based on linguistic features to analyze discourse structure information.

### 2.3 Extracting Social Networks from Text

Little work has been done on the front of extracting social relations between individuals from text. Elson et al. (2010) present a method for extracting social networks from nineteenth-century British novels and serials. They link two characters based on whether they are in conversation or not. McCallum et al. (2007) explored the use of structured data such as email headers for social network construction. Gruzd and Hyrthonthwaite (2008) explored the use of post text in discussions to study interaction patterns in e-learning communities.

Our work is related to this line of research because we employ natural language processing techniques to reveal embedded social structures. Despite similarities, our work is uniquely characterized by the fact that we extract signed social networks from text.

### 2.4 Signed Social Networks

Most of the work on social networks analysis has only focused on positive interactions. A few recent papers have taken the signs of edges into account.

Brzozowski et al. (2008) study the positive and negative relationships between users of Essembly. Essembly is an ideological social network that distinguishes between ideological allies and nemeses. Kunegis et al. (2009) analyze user relationships in the Slashdot technology news site. Slashdot allows users of the website to tag other users as friends or foes, providing positive and negative endorsements. Leskovec et al. (2010c) study signed social networks generated from Slashdot, Epinions, and Wikipedia. They also connect their analysis to theories of signed networks from social psychology. A similar study used the same datasets for predicting positive and negative links given their context (Leskovec et al., 2010a). Other work addressed the problem of clustering signed networks by taking both positive and negative edges into consideration (Yang et al., 2007; Doreian and Mrvar, 2009).

All this work has been limited to analyzing a handful of datasets for which an explicit notion of both positive and negative relations exists. Our work goes beyond this limitation by leveraging the power of natural language processing to automate the discovery of signed social networks using the text embedded in the network.

## 3 Approach

The general goal of this work is to mine attitude between individuals engaged in an online discussion. We use that to extract a signed social network representing the interactions between different participants. Our approach consists of several steps. In this section, we will explain how we identify sentiment at the word level (i.e. polarity), at the sentence level (i.e. attitude), and finally generalize over this to find positive/negative interactions between individuals based on their text correspondences.

The first step toward identifying attitude is to identify polarized words. Polarized words are very good indicators of subjective sentences and hence we their existence will be highly correlated with the existence of attitude. The method we use for identifying word polarity is a Random Walk based method over a word relatedness graph (Hassan and Radev, 2010).

The following step is to move to the sentence level by examining different sentences to find out which sentences display an attitude from the text writer to the recipient. We train a classifier based on several sources of information to make this prediction (Hassan et al., 2010). We use lexical items, polarity tags, part-of-speech tags, and dependency parse trees to train a classifier that identifies sentences with attitude.

Finally, we build a network connecting participants based on their interactions. We use the predictions we made both at the word and sentence levels to associate a sign to every edge.

### 3.1 Identified Positive/Negative Words

The first step toward identifying attitude is to identify words with positive/negative semantic orientation. The semantic orientation or polarity of a word indicates the direction the word deviates from the norm (Lehrer, 1974). Past work has demonstrated that polarized words are very good indicators of subjective sentences (Hatzivassiloglou and Wiebe, 2000; Wiebe et al., 2001). We use a Random Walk based method to identify the semantic orientation of words (Hassan and Radev, 2010). We construct a graph where each node represents a word/part-of-speech pair. We connect nodes based on synonyms, hypernyms, and similar-to relations from WordNet (Miller, 1995). For words that do not appear in WordNet, we use distributional similarity (Lee, 1999) as a proxy for word relatedness.

We use a list of words with known polarity (Stone et al., 1966) to label some of the nodes in the graph. We then define a random walk model where the set of nodes correspond to the state space, and transition probabilities are estimated by normalizing edge weights. We assume that a random surfer walks along the word relatedness graph starting from a word with unknown polarity. The walk continues until the surfer hits a word with a known polarity. Seed words with known polarity act as an absorbing boundary for the random walk. We calculate the mean hitting time (Norris, 1997) from any word with unknown polarity to the set of positive seeds and the set of negative seeds. If the absolute difference of the two mean hitting times is below a certain threshold, the word is classified as neutral. Otherwise, it is labeled with the class that has the smallest mean hitting time.

### 3.2 Identifying Attitude from Text

The first step toward identifying attitude is to identify words with positive/negative semantic orientation. The semantic orientation or polarity of a word indicates the direction the word deviates from the norm (Lehrer, 1974). We use OpinionFinder (Wilson et al., 2005a) to identify words with positive or negative semantic orientation. The polarity of a word is also affected by the context where the word appears. For example, a positive word that appears in a negated context should have a negative polarity. Other polarized words sometimes appear as neutral words in some contexts. Hence, we use the method described in (Wilson et al., 2005b) to identify the contextual polarity of words given their isolated polarity. A large set of features is used for that purpose including words, sentences, structure, and other features.

Our overall objective is to find the direct attitude between participants. Hence after identifying the semantic orientation of individual words, we move on to predicting which polarized expressions target the addressee and which are not.

Sentences that show an attitude are different from subjective sentences. Subjective sentences are sentences used to express opinions, evaluations, and speculations (Riloff and Wiebe, 2003). While every sentence that shows an attitude is a subjective sentence, not every subjective sentence shows an attitude toward the recipient. A discussion sentence may display an opinion about any topic yet no attitude.

We address the problem of identifying sentences with attitude as a relation detection problem in a supervised learning setting (Hassan et al., 2010). We study sentences that use second person pronouns and polarized expressions. We predict whether the second person pronoun is related to the polarized expression or not. We regard the second person pronoun and the polarized expression as two entities and try to learn a classifier that predicts whether the two entities are related or not. The text connecting the two entities offers a very condensed representation of the information needed to assess whether they are related or not. For example the two sentences "you are completely unqualified" and "you know what, he is unqualified ..." show two different ways the words "you", and "unqualified" could appear in a sentence. In the first case the polarized word unqualified refers to the word you. In the second case, the two words are not related. The sequence of words connecting the two entities is a very good predictor for whether they are related or not. However, these paths are completely lexicalized and consequently their performance will be limited by data sparseness. To alleviate this problem, we use higher levels of generalization to represent the path connecting the two tokens. These representations are the part-of-speech tags, and the shortest path in a dependency graph connecting the two tokens. We represent every sentence with several representations at different levels of generalization. For example, the sentence your ideas are very inspiring will be represented using lexical, polarity, part-of-speech, and dependency information as follows:

LEX: "*YOUR ideas are very POS*"
POS: "*YOUR NNS VBP RB JJ_POS*"
DEP: "*YOUR poss nsubj POS*"

#### 3.2.1 A Text Classification Approach

In this method, we treat the problem as a topic classification problem with two topics: having positive attitude and having negative attitude. As we are only interested in attitude between participants rather than sentiment in general, we restrict the text we analyze to sentences that contain mentions of the addressee (e.g. name or second person pronouns). A similar approach for sentiment classification has been presented in (Pang et al., ).

We represent text using the popular bag-of-words approach. Every piece of text is represented using a high dimensional feature space. Every word is considered a feature. The *tf-idf* weighting schema is used to calculate feature weights. *tf*, or term frequency, is the number of time a term $t$ occurred in a document $d$. *idf*, or inverse document frequency, is a measure of the general importance of the term. It is obtained by dividing the total number of documents by the number of documents containing the term. The logarithm of this value is often used instead of the original value.

We used Support Vector Machines (SVMs) for classification. SVM has been shown to be highly effective for traditional text classification. We used the SVM Light implementation with default parameters (Joachims, 1999). All stop words were removed and all documents were length normalized before training.

The set of features we use are the set of unigrams, and bigrams representing the words, part-of-speech tags, and dependency relations connecting the two entities. For example the following features will be set for the previous example:

YOUR_ideas, YOUR_NNS, YOUR_poss, poss_nsubj, ...., etc.

We use Support Vector Machines (SVM) as a learning system because it is good with handling high dimensional feature spaces.

### 3.3 Extracting the Signed Network

In this subsection, we describe the procedure we used to build the signed network given the components we described in the previous subsections. This procedure consists of two main steps. The first is building the network without signs, and the second is assigning signs to different edges.

To build the network, we parse our data to identify different threads, posts and senders. Every sender is represented with a node in the network. An edge connects two nodes if there exists an interaction between the corresponding participants. We add a directed edge $A \rightarrow B$, if $A$ replies to $B$'s posts at least $n$ times in $m$ different threads. We set $m$, and $n$ to 2 in most of our experiments. The interaction information (i.e. who replies to whom) can be extracted directly from the thread structure.

Once we build the network, we move to the more challenging task in which we associate a sign with every edge. We have shown in the previous section how sentences with positive and negative attitude can be extracted from text. Unfortunately the sign of an interaction cannot be trivially inferred from the polarity of sentences. For example, a single negative sentence written by $A$ and directed to $B$ does not mean that the interaction between $A$ and $B$ is negative. One way to solve this problem would be to compare the number of negative sentences to positive sentences in all posts between $A$ and $B$ and classify the interaction according to the plurality value. We will show later, in our experiment section, that such a simplistic method does not perform well in predicting the sign of an interaction.

As a result, we decided to pose the problem as a classical supervised learning problem. We came up with a set of features that we think are good predictors of the interaction sign, and we train a classifier using those features on a labeled dataset. Our features include numbers and percentages of positive/negative sentences per post, posts per thread, and so on. A sentence is labeled as positive/negative if a relation has been detected in this sentence between a second person pronoun and a positive/negative expression. A post is considered positive/negative based on the majority of relations detected in it. We use two sets of features. The first set is related to $A$ only or $B$ only. The second set

| Participant Features |
|---|
| Number of posts per month for A (B) |
| Percentage of positive posts per month for A (B) |
| Percentage of negative posts per month for A (B) |
| gender |
| **Interaction Features** |
| Percentage/number of positive (negative) sentences per post |
| Percentage/number of positive (negative) posts per thread |
| Discussion Topic |

Table 1: Features used by the Interaction Sign Classifier.

| Class | Pos. | Neg. | Weigh. Avg. |
|---|---|---|---|
| TP Rate | 0.847 | 0.809 | 0.835 |
| FP Rate | 0.191 | 0.153 | 0.179 |
| Precision | 0.906 | 0.71 | 0.844 |
| Recall | 0.847 | 0.809 | 0.835 |
| F-Measure | 0.875 | 0.756 | 0.838 |
| Accuracy | - | - | **0.835** |

Table 2: Interaction sign classifier evaluation.

is related to the interactions between $A$ and $B$. The features are outlined in Table 1.

## 4 Data

Our data consists of a large amount of discussion threads collected from online discussion forums. We collected around $41,000$ threads and $1.2$M posts from the period between the end of 2008 and the end of 2010. All threads were in English and had 5 posts or more. They covered a wide range of topics including: politics, religion, science, etc. The data was tokenized, sentence-split, and part-of-speech tagged with the OpenNLP toolkit. It was parsed with the Stanford parser (Klein and Manning, 2003).

We randomly selected $5300$ posts (having approximately $1000$ interactions), and asked human annotators to label them. Our annotators were instructed to read all the posts exchanged between two participants and decide whether the interaction between them is positive or negative. We used Amazon Mechanical Turk for annotations. Following previous work (Callison-Burch, 2009; Akkaya et al., 2010), we took several precautions to maintain data integrity. We restricted annotators to those based in the US to maintain an acceptable level of English fluency. We also restricted annotators to those who have more than 95% approval rate for all previous work. Moreover, we asked three different annotators to label every interaction. The label was computed by taking the majority vote among the three annotators. We refer to this data as the *Interactions Dataset*.

The kappa measure between the three groups of annotations was $0.62$. To better assess the quality of the annotations, we asked a trained annotator to label 10% of the data. We measured the agreement between the expert annotator and the majority label from the Mechanical Turk. The kappa measure was $0.69$.

We trained the classifier that detects sentences with attitude (Section 3.1) on a set of $4000$ manually annotated sentences. None of this data overlaps with the dataset described earlier. A similar annotation procedure was used to label this data. We refer to this data as the *Sentences Dataset*.

## 5 Results and Discussion

We performed experiments on the data described in the previous section. We trained and tested the sentence with attitude detection classifiers described in Section 3.1 using the *Sentences Dataset*. We also trained and tested the interaction sign classifier described in Section 3.3 using the *Interactions Dataset*. We build one unsigned network from every topic in the data set. This results in a signed social network for every topic (e.g. politics, economics,etc.). We decided to build a network for every topic as opposed to one single network because the relation between any two individuals may vary across topics. In the rest of this section, we will describe the experiments we did to assess the performance of the sentences with attitude detection and interaction sign prediction steps.

In addition to classical evaluation, we evaluate our results using the structural balance theory which has been shown to hold both theoretically (Heider, 1946) and empirically (Leskovec et al., 2010b). We validate our results by showing that the *automatically* extracted networks mostly agree with the theory.

### 5.1 Identifying Sentences with Attitude

We tested this component using the *Sentences Dataset* described in Section 4. In a 10-fold cross validation mode, the classifier achieves 80.3% accuracy, 81.0% precision, %79.4 recall, and 80.2% F1.

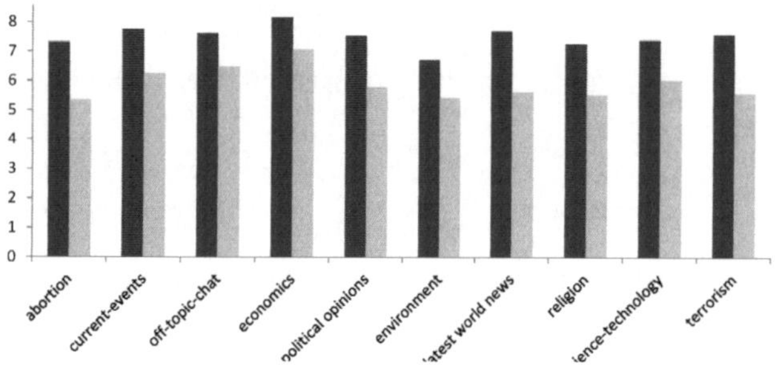


Figure 1: Percentage of balanced triangles in extracted network vs. random network.

## 5.2 Interaction Sign Classifier

We used the relation detection classifier described in Section 3.2 to find sentences with positive and negative attitude. The output of this classifier was used to compute the the features described in Section 3.3, which were used to train a classifier that predicts the sign of an interaction between any two individuals.

We used Support Vector Machines (SVM) to train the sign interaction classifier. We report several performance metrics for them in Table 2. All results were computed using 10 fold cross validation on the labeled data. To better assess the performance of the proposed classifier, we compare it to a baseline that labels the relation as negative if the percentage of negative sentences exceeds a particular threshold, otherwise it is labeled as positive. The thresholds was empirically evaluated using a separate development set. The accuracy of this baseline is only 71%.

We evaluated the importance of the features listed in Table 1 by measuring the chi-squared statistic for every feature with respect to the class. We found out that the features describing the interaction between the two participants are more informative than the ones describing individuals characteristics. The later features are still helpful though and they improve the performance by a statistically significant amount. We also noticed that all features based on percentages are more informative than those based on count. The most informative features are: percentage of negative posts per tread, percentage of negative sentences per post, percentage of positive posts per thread, number of negative posts, and discussion topic.

## 5.3 Structural Balance Theory

The structural balance theory is a psychological theory that tries to explain the dynamics of signed social interactions. It has been shown to hold both theoretically (Heider, 1946) and empirically (Leskovec et al., 2010b). In this section, we study the agreement between the theory and the *automatically* extracted networks. The theory has its origins in the work of Heider (1946). It was then formalized in a graph theoretic form in (Cartwright and Harary, ). The theory is based on the principles that "the friend of my friend is my friend", "the enemy of my friend is my enemy", "the friend of my enemy is my enemy", and variations on these.

There are several possible ways in which triangles representing the relation of three people can be signed. The structural balance theory states that triangles that have an odd number of positive signs (+ + + and + - -) are balanced, while triangles that have an even number of positive signs (- - - and + + -) are not.

Even though the structural balance theory posits some triangles as unbalanced, that does not eliminate the chance of their existence. Actually, for most observed signed structures for social groups, exact structural balance does not hold (Doreian and Mrvar, 1996). Davis (1967) developed the theory further into the *weak structural balance theory*. In this theory, he extended the structural balance theory to cases where there can be more than two such mutually antagonistic subgroups. Hence, he suggested that only triangles with exactly two positive edges are implausible in real networks, and that all other kinds of triangles should be permissible.

In this section, we connect our analysis to the structural balance theory. We compare the predictions of edge signs made by our system to the structural balance theory by counting the frequencies of different types of triangles in the predicted network. Showing that our automatically constructed network agrees with the structural balance theory further validates our results.

We compute the frequency of every type of triangle for ten different topics. We compare these frequencies to the frequencies of triangles in a set of random networks. We shuffle signs for all edges on every network keeping the fractions of positive and

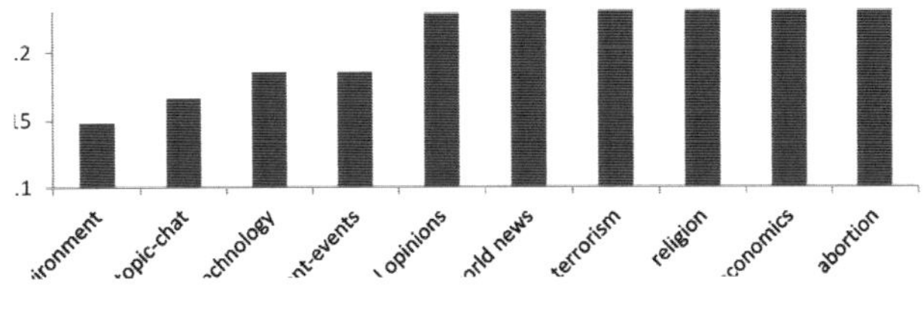


Figure 2: Percentage of negative edges across topics.

negative edges constant.

We repeat shuffling for 1000 times. Every time, we compute the frequencies of different types of triangles. We find that the all-positive triangle $(+++)$ is overrepresented in the generated network compared to chance across all topics. We also see that the triangle with two positive edges $(++-)$, and the all-negative triangle $(---)$ are underrepresented compared to chance across all topics. The triangle with a single positive edge is slightly overrepresented in most but not all of the topics compared to chance. This shows that the predicted networks mostly agree with the structural balance theory. In general, the percentage of balanced triangles in the predicted networks is higher than in the shuffled networks, and hence the balanced triangles are significantly overrepresented compared to chance. Figure 1 compares the percentage of balanced triangles in the predicted networks and the shuffled networks. This proves that our *automatically* constructed network is similar to explicit signed networks in that they both mostly agree with the balance theory.

## 6 Application: Dispute Level Prediction

There are many applications that could benefit from the signed network representation of discussions such as community finding, stance recognition, recommendation systems, and disputed topics identification. In this section, we will describe one such application.

Discussion forums usually respond quickly to new topics and events. Some of those topics usually receive more attention and more dispute than others. We can identify such topics and in general measure the amount of dispute every topic receives using the extracted signed network. We computed the percentage of negative edges to all edges for every topic. We believe that this would act as a measure for how disputed a particular topic is. We see, from Figure 2, that "environment", "science", and "technology" topics are among the least disputed topics, whereas "terrorism", "abortion" and "economics" are among the most disputed topics. These findings are another way of validating our predictions. They also suggest another application for this work that focuses on measuring the amount of dispute different topics receive. This can be done for more specific topics, rather than high level topics as shown here, to identify hot topics that receive a lot of dispute.

## 7 Conclusions

In this paper, we have shown that natural language processing techniques can be reliably used to extract signed social networks from text correspondences. We believe that this work brings us closer to understanding the relation between language use and social interactions and opens the door to further research efforts that go beyond standard social network analysis by studying the interplay of positive and negative connections. We rigorously evaluated the proposed methods on labeled data and connected our analysis to social psychology theories to show that our predictions mostly agree with them. Finally, we presented potential applications that benefit from the automatically extracted signed network.

## References


Cem Akkaya, Alexander Conrad, Janyce Wiebe, and Rada Mihalcea. 2010. Amazon mechanical turk for subjectivity word sense disambiguation. In *CSLDAMT '10*.

Carmen Banea, Rada Mihalcea, and Janyce Wiebe. 2008. A bootstrapping method for building subjectivity lexicons for languages with scarce resources. In *LREC'08*.

Michael J. Brzozowski, Tad Hogg, and Gabor Szabo. 2008. Friends and foes: ideological social networking. In *SIGCHI*.

Chris Callison-Burch. 2009. Fast, cheap, and creative: evaluating translation quality using amazon's mechanical turk. In *EMNLP '9*, EMNLP '09.

Dorwin Cartwright and Frank Harary. Structure balance: A generalization of heiders theory. *Psych. Rev.*

J. A. Davis. 1967. Clustering and structural balance in graphs. *Human Relations*.

Patrick Doreian and Andrej Mrvar. 1996. A partitioning approach to structural balance. *Social Networks*.

Patrick Doreian and Andrej Mrvar. 2009. Partitioning signed social networks. *Social Networks.*

David Elson, Nicholas Dames, and Kathleen McKeown. 2010. Extracting social networks from literary fiction. In *ACL 2010*, Uppsala, Sweden.

Anatoliy Gruzd and Caroline Haythornthwaite. 2008. Automated discovery and analysis of social networks from threaded discussions. In *(INSNA)*.

Ahmed Hassan and Dragomir Radev. 2010. Identifying text polarity using random walks. In *ACL'10.*

Ahmed Hassan, Vahed Qazvinian, and Dragomir Radev. 2010. What's with the attitude?: identifying sentences with attitude in online discussions. In *Proceedings of the 2010 Conference on Empirical Methods in Natural Language Processing*.

V. Hatzivassiloglou and K. McKeown. 1997. Predicting the semantic orientation of adjectives. In *EACL'97.*

Vasileios Hatzivassiloglou and Janyce Wiebe. 2000. Effects of adjective orientation and gradability on sentence subjectivity. In *COLING.*

Fritz Heider. 1946. Attitudes and cognitive organization. *Journal of Psychology.*

J. Huang, M. Zhou, and D. Yang. 2007. Extracting chatbot knowledge from online discussion forums. In *IJ-CAI'07.*

Thorsten Joachims, 1999. *Making large-scale support vector machine learning practical.* MIT Press.

Dan Klein and Christopher D. Manning. 2003. Accurate unlexicalized parsing. In *ACL'03.*

Jérôme Kunegis, Andreas Lommatzsch, and Christian Bauckhage. 2009. The slashdot zoo: mining a social network with negative edges. In *WWW '09.*

Lillian Lee. 1999. Measures of distributional similarity. In *ACL-1999.*

A. Lehrer. 1974. Semantic fields and lezical structure.

Jure Leskovec, Daniel Huttenlocher, and Jon Kleinberg. 2010a. Predicting positive and negative links in online social networks. In *WWW '10.*

Jure Leskovec, Daniel Huttenlocher, and Jon Kleinberg. 2010b. Signed networks in social media. In *CHI 2010.*

Jure Leskovec, Daniel Huttenlocher, and Jon Kleinberg. 2010c. Signed networks in social media. In *Proceedings of the 28th international conference on Human factors in computing systems*, pages 1361–1370, New York, NY, USA.

Chen Lin, Jiang-Ming Yang, Rui Cai, Xin-Jing Wang, and Wei Wang. 2009. Simultaneously modeling semantics and structure of threaded discussions: a sparse coding approach and its applications. In *SIGIR '09.*

Andrew McCallum, Xuerui Wang, and Andrés Corrada-Emmanuel. 2007. Topic and role discovery in social networks with experiments on enron and academic email. *J. Artif. Int. Res.*, 30:249–272, October.

George A. Miller. 1995. Wordnet: a lexical database for english. *Commun. ACM.*

Tetsuya Nasukawa and Jeonghee Yi. 2003. Sentiment analysis: capturing favorability using natural language processing. In *K-CAP '03.*

J. Norris. 1997. Markov chains. Cambridge University Press.

Bo Pang, Lillian Lee, and Shivakumar Vaithyanathan. Thumbs up?: sentiment classification using machine learning techniques. In *EMNLP*. Association for Computational Linguistics.

A. Popescu and O. Etzioni. 2005. Extracting product features and opinions from reviews. In *HLT-EMNLP'05.*

E. Riloff and J. Wiebe. 2003. Learning extraction patterns for subjective expressions. In *EMNLP'03.*

Dou Shen, Qiang Yang, Jian-Tao Sun, and Zheng Chen. 2006. Thread detection in dynamic text message streams. In *SIGIR '06*, pages 35–42.

Philip Stone, Dexter Dunphy, Marchall Smith, and Daniel Ogilvie. 1966. The general inquirer: A computer approach to content analysis. *The MIT Press.*

Hiroya Takamura, Takashi Inui, and Manabu Okumura. 2005. Extracting semantic orientations of words using spin model. In *ACL'05.*

P. Turney and M. Littman. 2003. Measuring praise and criticism: Inference of semantic orientation from association. *Transactions on Information Systems.*

Janyce Wiebe, Rebecca Bruce, Matthew Bell, Melanie Martin, and Theresa Wilson. 2001. A corpus study of evaluative and speculative language. In *Proceedings of the Second SIGdial Workshop on Discourse and Dialogue*, pages 1–10.

Janyce Wiebe. 2000. Learning subjective adjectives from corpora. In *AAAI-IAAI.*

Theresa Wilson, Paul Hoffmann, Swapna Somasundaran, Jason Kessler, Janyce Wiebe, Yejin Choi, Claire Cardie, Ellen Riloff, and Siddharth Patwardhan. 2005a. Opinionfinder: a system for subjectivity analysis. In *HLT/EMNLP.*

Theresa Wilson, Janyce Wiebe, and Paul Hoffmann. 2005b. Recognizing contextual polarity in phrase-level sentiment analysis. In *HLT/EMNLP'05.*

Bo Yang, William Cheung, and Jiming Liu. 2007. Community mining from signed social networks. *IEEE Trans. on Knowl. and Data Eng.*, 19(10).

Hong Yu and Vasileios Hatzivassiloglou. 2003. Towards answering opinion questions: separating facts from opinions and identifying the polarity of opinion sentences. In *EMNLP'03.*

# Using Link Analysis to Discover Interesting Messages Spread Across Twitter

**Min-Chul Yang**[†] and **Jung-Tae Lee**[‡] and **Hae-Chang Rim**[†]
[†]Dept. of Computer & Radio Communications Engineering, Korea University, Seoul, Korea
[‡]Research Institute of Computer Information & Communication, Korea University, Seoul, Korea
{mcyang, jtlee, rim}@nlp.korea.ac.kr

## Abstract

Twitter, a popular social networking service, enables its users to not only send messages but re-broadcast or *retweet* a message from another Twitter user to their own followers. Considering the number of times that a message is retweeted across Twitter is a straightforward way to estimate how interesting it is. However, a considerable number of messages in Twitter with high retweet counts are actually mundane posts by celebrities that are of interest to themselves and possibly their followers. In this paper, we leverage retweets as implicit relationships between Twitter users and messages and address the problem of automatically finding messages in Twitter that may be of potential interest to a wide audience by using link analysis methods that look at more than just the sheer number of retweets. Experimental results on real world data demonstrate that the proposed method can achieve better performance than several baseline methods.

## 1 Introduction

Twitter (`http://twitter.com`) is a popular social networking and microblogging service that enables its users to share their status updates, news, observations, and findings in real-time by posting text-based messages of up to 140 characters, called *tweets*. The service rapidly gained worldwide popularity as a communication tool, with millions of users generating millions of tweets per day. Although many of those tweets contain valuable information that is of interest to many people, many others are mundane tweets, such as *"Thanks guys for the birthday wishes!!"* that are of interest only to the authors and users who subscribed to their tweets, known as *followers*. Finding tweets that are of potential interest to a wide audience from large volume of tweets being accumulated in real-time is a crucial but challenging task. One straightforward way is to rely on the numbers of times each tweet has been propagated or *retweeted* by readers of the tweet. Hong et al. (2011) propose to regard retweet count as a measure of popularity and present classifiers for predicting whether and how often new tweets will be retweeted in the future. However, mundane tweets by highly popular users, such as celebrities with huge numbers of followers, can record high retweet counts. Alonso et al. (2010) use crowdsourcing to categorize a set of tweets as "only interesting to author and friends" and "possibly interesting to others" and report that the presence of a URL link is a single, highly effective feature for distinguishing interesting tweets with more than 80% accuracy. This simple rule, however, may incorrectly recognize many interesting tweets as not interesting, simply because they do not contain links. Lauw et al. (2010) suggest several features for identifying interesting tweets but do not experimentally validate them.

In this study, we follow the definition of interesting tweets provided by Alonso et al. (2010) and focus on automatic methods for finding tweets that may be of potential interest to not only the authors and their followers but a wider audience. Since retweets are intended to spread tweets to new audiences, they are often a recommendation or, according to Boyd et al. (2010), productive communication tool. Thus, we model Twitter as a graph consisting of user and tweet nodes implicitly connected by retweet links, each of which is formed when one user retweets what another user tweeted. We present a variant of the popular HITS algorithm (Kleinberg, 1999) that exploits the retweet link structure as an indicator of how interesting an individual tweet is. Specifically, we draw attention on the fact that not all retweets are meaningful. Some users retweet a message, not because of its content, but only because they were asked to, or because they regard retweeting as an act of friendship, loyalty, or homage towards the person who originally tweeted (Boyd et al., 2010). The algorithm proposed in this paper is designed upon the premise that not all retweet links are created equal, assuming that some retweets may carry more importance or weight than others. Welch et al. (2011) and Romero et al. (2011) similarly extend link analysis to Twitter, but address essentially different problems. We conduct experiments on real world tweet data and demonstrate that our method achieves better performance than the simple retweet count approach and a similar recent work on Twitter messages (Castillo et al., 2011) that uses supervised learning with a broad spectrum of features.

## 2 Proposed Method

We treat the problem of finding interesting tweets as a ranking problem where the goal is to derive a scoring function which gives higher scores to interesting tweets than to uninteresting ones in a given set of tweets. To derive the scoring function, we adopt a variant of HITS, a popular link analysis method that emphasizes mutual reinforcement between authority and hub nodes (Kleinberg, 1999).

Formally, we model the Twitter structure as directed graph $G = (N, E)$ with nodes $N$ and directional edges $E$. We consider both users $U = \{u_1, \ldots, u_{n_u}\}$ and tweets $T = \{t_1, \ldots, t_{n_t}\}$ as nodes and the retweet relations between these nodes as directional edges. For instance, if tweet $t_a$, created by user $u_a$, retweets $t_b$, written by user $u_b$, we create a retweet edge $e_{t_a,t_b}$ from $t_a$ to $t_b$ and another retweet edge $e_{u_a,u_b}$ from $u_a$ to $u_b$.[1] Strictly speaking, $G$ has two subgraphs, one based only on the user nodes and another based on the tweet nodes. Instead of running HITS on the tweet subgraph right away, we first run it on the user subgraph and let tweets inherit the scores from their publishers. Our premise is that the scores of a user is an important prior information to infer the scores of the tweets that the user published.

**User-level procedure**: We first run the algorithm on the user subgraph. $\forall u_i$, we update the authority scores $A(u_i)$ as:

$$\sum_{\forall j: e_{u_j,u_i} \in E} \frac{|\{u_k \in U : e_{u_j,u_k} \in E\}|}{|\{k : e_{u_j,u_k} \in E\}|} \times H(u_j) \quad (1)$$

Then, $\forall u_i$, we update the hub scores $H(u_i)$ to be:

$$\sum_{\forall j: e_{u_i,u_j} \in E} \frac{|\{u_k \in U : e_{u_k,u_j} \in E\}|}{|\{k : e_{u_k,u_j} \in E\}|} \times A(u_j) \quad (2)$$

A series of iterations is performed until the scores are converged. After each iteration, the authority/hub scores are normalized by dividing each of them by the square root of the sum of the squares of all authority/hub values. When this user-level stage ends, the algorithm outputs a function $S_{U_A} : U \rightarrow [0, 1]$, which represents the user's final authority score, and another function $S_{U_H} : U \rightarrow [0, 1]$, which outputs the user's final hub score. Note that, unlike the standard HITS, the authority/hub scores are influenced by edge weights that reflect the retweet behaviors of individual users. The idea here is to dampen the influence of users who devote most of their retweet activities toward a very few other users, such as celebrities, and increase the weight of users who retweet many different users' tweets. To demonstrate the effectiveness of the parameter, we have done some preliminary experiments. The column User$_{from}$ in Table 1 shows the retweet behavior of users who retweeted tweets belonging to "uninteresting" and "interesting" classes observed in our Twitter dataset. The values are calculated by the ratio of all other users that a user retweeted to all retweet outlinks from the user; a value closer to 1 means that outlinks are pointed to many different users.[2] We observe that the value for users who retweeted interesting tweets is shown to be higher, which means that they tend to retweet messages from many different users, more than users who retweeted uninteresting ones.

[1] Note that two user nodes can have multiple edges.

[2] For calculating the ratios, we limit the target to users who retweeted two or more times in our dataset.

| Class | User$_{from}$ | $F = \alpha$ | # |
|---|---|---|---|
| Not Interesting | 0.591 | 0.252 | 1985 |
| Possibly Interesting | 0.711 | 0.515 | 1115 |
| Both | 0.634 | 0.346 | 3100 |

Table 1: Dataset analysis.

**Tweet-level procedure**: After the user-level stage, we start computing the scores of the tweet nodes. In each iteration, we start out with each tweet node initially inheriting the scores of its publisher. Let $P : T \rightarrow U$ be a function that returns the publisher of a given tweet. $\forall t_i$, we update $A(t_i)$ to be:

$$S_{U_A}(P(t_i)) + \sum_{\forall j: e_{t_j,t_i} \in E} F(e_{t_j,t_i}) \times H(t_j) \quad (3)$$

Then, $\forall t_i$, we update $H(t_i)$ to be:

$$S_{U_H}(P(t_i)) + \sum_{\forall j: e_{t_i,t_j} \in E} F(e_{t_i,t_j}) \times A(t_j) \quad (4)$$

where $F(e_{t_a,t_b})$ is a parameter function that returns $\alpha > 1$ if $P(t_a)$ is not a follower of $P(t_b)$ and 1 otherwise. It is intuitive that if users retweet other users' tweets even if they are not friends, then it is more likely that those tweets are interesting. The column $F = \alpha$ in Table 1 shows the ratio of all unfollowers who retweeted messages in a particular class to all users who retweeted messages in that class, observed in our dataset. We observe that users retweet interesting messages more, even when they do not follow the publishers. Similar observation has also been made by Recuero et al. (2011). After each iteration, the authority/hub scores are normalized as done in the user-level. After performing several iterations until convergence, the algorithm finally outputs a scoring function $S_{T_A} : T \rightarrow [0, 1]$, which represents the tweet node's final authority score. We use this function to produce the final ranking of tweets.

**Text pattern rules**: We observe that in some cases users retweet messages from their friends, not because of the contents, but via retweet requests to simply evoke attention. To prevent useless tweets containing such requests from receiving high authority scores, we collect 20 simple text pattern matching rules that frequently appear in those tweets. Specifically, we let the rules make influence while updating the scores of tweets by modifying the summations in Eq. (3) and (4) respectively as:

$$\sum_{\forall j: e_{t_j,t_i} \in E} F(e_{t_j,t_i}) \times R(t_i) \times H(t_j) \quad (5)$$

$$\sum_{\forall j: e_{t_i,t_j} \in E} F(e_{t_i,t_j}) \times R(t_j) \times A(t_j) \quad (6)$$

where $R(t)$ is a rule-based function that returns 0 if tweet $t$ contains one of the pre-defined text patterns and 1 otherwise. Such patterns include *"RT this if"* and *"If this tweet gets RT * times I will"*.

## 3 Experiment and Discussion

Our Twitter dataset is collected during 31 days of October 2011, containing 64,107,169 tweets and 2,824,365 users. For evaluation, we generated 31 immediate Twitter graphs composed of 1.5 million retweet links in average and 31 initially ranked lists of tweets, each consisting of top 100 tweets created on a specific date of the month with highest retweet counts accumulated during the next 7 days. Two annotators were instructed to categorize each tweet as interesting or not, by inspecting its content as done in the work of Alonso et al. (2010). In case of disagreement (about 15% of all cases), a final judgment was made by consensus between the two annotators. We observe that the ratio of tweets judged to be interesting is about 36%; the column '#' in Table 1 shows the actual counts of each class. The goal of this evaluation is to demonstrate that our method is able to produce better ranked lists of tweets by re-ranking interesting tweets highly.

Table 2 reports the ranking performance of various methods in terms of Precisions @10 and @20, R-Precision, and MAP. We compare our approach to four baselines. The first baseline, #RT, is obviously based on retweet counts; tweets with higher retweet counts are ranked higher. The second baseline, #URL+#RT, favors tweets that contain URL links (Alonso et al., 2010). Since it is less likely for a tweet to contain more than one link, we additionally use #RT to break ties in tweet ranking. Thirdly, HITS$_{original}$, is the standard HITS algorithm run on both user and tweet subgraphs that calculates authority/hub scores of a node purely by the sum of hub values that point to it and the sum of authority values that it points to, respectively, during iterations;

| Method | P@10 | P@20 | R-Prec | MAP |
|---|---|---|---|---|
| #RT | 0.294 | 0.313 | 0.311 | 0.355 |
| #URL+#RT | 0.245 | 0.334 | 0.362 | 0.361 |
| $\text{HITS}_{original}$ | 0.203 | 0.387 | 0.478 | 0.465 |
| $\text{ML}_{message}$ | 0.671 | 0.645 | 0.610 | 0.642 |
| $\text{ML}_{all}$ | 0.819 | 0.795 | 0.698 | 0.763 |
| $\text{HITS}_{proposed}$ | **0.881** | **0.829** | **0.744** | **0.807** |

Table 2: Performance of individual methods

| Method | P@10 | P@20 | R-Prec | MAP |
|---|---|---|---|---|
| $\text{HITS}_{proposed}$ | **0.881** | **0.829** | **0.744** | **0.807** |
| *w/o* User | 0.677 | 0.677 | 0.559 | 0.591 |
| *w/o* Tweet | 0.861 | 0.779 | 0.702 | 0.772 |
| *w/o* Rule | 0.858 | 0.81 | 0.733 | 0.781 |

Table 3: Contributions of individual stages.

no other influential factors are considered in the calculations. Lastly, we choose one recent work by Castillo et al. (2011) that addresses a related problem to ours, which aims at learning to classify tweets as credible or not credible. Although interestingness and credibility are two distinct concepts, the work presents a wide range of features that may be applied for assessing interestingness of tweets using machine learning. For re-implementation, we train a binary SVM classifier using features proposed by Castillo et al. (2011), which include features from users' tweet and retweet behavior, the text of the tweets, and citations to external sources; we use the probability estimates of the learned classifier for re-ranking.[3] We use leave-one-out cross validation in order to evaluate this last approach, denoted as $\text{ML}_{all}$. $\text{ML}_{message}$ is a variant that relies only on message-based features of tweets. Our method, with $\alpha$ empirically set to 7, is denoted as $\text{HITS}_{proposed}$.

We observe that #RT alone is not sufficient measure for discovering interesting tweets. Additionally leveraging #URL helps, but the improvements are only marginal. By manually inspecting tweets with both high retweet counts and links, it is revealed that many of them were tweets from celebrities with links to their self-portraits photographed in their daily lives, which may be of interest to their own followers only. $\text{HITS}_{original}$ performs better than both #RT and #URL across most evaluation metrics but generally does not demonstrate good performance. $\text{ML}_{message}$ always outperform the first three significantly; we observe that tweet lengths in characters and in words are the two most effective message-based features for finding interesting tweets. The results of $\text{ML}_{all}$ demonstrates that more reasonable performance can be achieved when user- and propagation-based features are combined with message-based features. The proposed method significantly outperforms all the baselines. This is a significant result in that our method is an unsupervised approach that relies on a few number of tweet features and does not require complex training.

We lastly report the contribution of individual procedures in our algorithm in Table 3 by ablating each of the stages at a time. "*w/o User*" is when tweet nodes do not initially inherit the scores of their publishers. "*w/o Tweet*" is when tweets are re-ranked according to the authority scores of their publishers. "*w/o Rule*" is when we use Eq. (3) and (4) instead of Eq. (5) and (6) for updating tweet scores. We observe that the user-level procedure plays the most crucial role. We believe this is because of the ability of HITS to distinguish good "hub-users". Since authoritative users can post ordinary status updates occasionally in Twitter, we cannot always expect them to create interesting content every time they tweet. However, good hub-users[4] tend to continuously spot and retweet interesting messages; thus, we can expect the tweets they share to be interesting steadily. The role of hubs is not as revealed on the tweet side of the Twitter graph, since each tweet node can only have at most one retweet outlink. The exclusion of text pattern rules does not harm the overall performance much. We suspect this is because of the small number of rules and expect more improvement if we add more effective rules.

## Acknowledgments

This work was supported by the Ministry of Knowledge Economy of Korea, under the title "Development of social web issue detection-monitoring & prediction technology for big data analytic listening platform of web intelligence (10039158)".

[3]We do not use some topic-based features in (Castillo et al., 2011) since such information is not available in our case.

[4]Often referred to as *content curators* (Bhargava, 2009).

## References

Omar Alonso, Chad Carson, David Gerster, Xiang Ji, and Shubha U. Nabar. 2010. Detecting uninteresting content in text streams. In *Proceedings of the SIGIR 2010 Workshop on Crowdsourcing for Search Evaluation*, CSE '10, pages 39–42.

Rohit Bhargava. 2009. Manifesto for the content curator: The next big social media job of the future? `http://rohitbhargava.typepad.com/`.

Danah Boyd, Scott Golder, and Gilad Lotan. 2010. Tweet, tweet, retweet: Conversational aspects of retweeting on twitter. In *Proceedings of the 2010 43rd Hawaii International Conference on System Sciences*, HICSS '10, pages 1–10.

Carlos Castillo, Marcelo Mendoza, and Barbara Poblete. 2011. Information credibility on twitter. In *Proceedings of the 20th international conference on World wide web*, WWW '11, pages 675–684.

Liangjie Hong, Ovidiu Dan, and Brian D. Davison. 2011. Predicting popular messages in twitter. In *Proceedings of the 20th international conference companion on World wide web*, WWW '11, pages 57–58.

Jon M. Kleinberg. 1999. Authoritative sources in a hyperlinked environment. *J. ACM*, 46(5):604–632.

Hady W. Lauw, Alexandros Ntoulas, and Krishnaram Kenthapadi. 2010. Estimating the quality of postings in the real-time web. In *Proceedings of the WSDM 2010 Workshop on Search in Social Media*, SSM '10.

Raquel Recuero, Ricardo Araujo, and Gabriela Zago. 2011. How does social capital affect retweets? In *Proceedings of the 5th International AAAI Conference on Weblogs and Social Media*, ICWSM '11, pages 305–312.

Daniel M. Romero, Wojciech Galuba, Sitaram Asur, and Bernardo A. Huberman. 2011. Influence and passivity in social media. In *Proceedings of the 2011 European Conference on Machine Learning and Principles and Practice of Knowledge Discovery in Databases*, ECML-PKDD '11, pages 18–33.

Michael J. Welch, Uri Schonfeld, Dan He, and Junghoo Cho. 2011. Topical semantics of twitter links. In *Proceedings of the 4th International Conference on Web Search and Web Data Mining*, WSDM '11, pages 327–336.

# Graph Based Similarity Measures for Synonym Extraction from Parsed Text

**Einat Minkov**
Dep. of Information Systems
University of Haifa
Haifa 31905, Israel
einatm@is.haifa.ac.il

**William W. Cohen**
School of Computer Science
Carnegie Mellon University
Pittsburgh, PA 15213
wcohen@cs.cmu.edu

## Abstract

We learn graph-based similarity measures for the task of extracting word synonyms from a corpus of parsed text. A constrained graph walk variant that has been successfully applied in the past in similar settings is shown to outperform a state-of-the-art syntactic vector-based approach on this task. Further, we show that learning specialized similarity measures for different word types is advantageous.

## 1 Introduction

Many applications of natural language processing require measures of lexico-semantic similarity. Examples include summarization (Barzilay and Elhadad, 1999), question answering (Lin and Pantel, 2001), and textual entailment (Mirkin et al., 2006). Graph-based methods have been successfully applied to evaluate word similarity using available ontologies, where the underlying graph included word senses and semantic relationships between them (Hughes and Ramage, 2007). Another line of research aims at eliciting semantic similarity measures directly from freely available corpora, based on the *distributional similarity* assumption (Harria, 1968). In this domain, vector-space methods give state-of-the-art performance (Padó and Lapata, 2007).

Previously, a graph based framework has been proposed that models word semantic similarity from parsed text (Minkov and Cohen, 2008). The underlying graph in this case describes a text corpus as connected dependency structures, according to the schema shown in Figure 1. The toy graph shown includes the dependency analysis of two sentences: "a major environmental disaster is under way", and "combat the environmental catastrophe". In the graph, word mentions (in circles) and word types (in squares) are both represented as nodes. Each word mention is linked to its corresponding word type; for example, the nodes "environmental$^3$" and "environmental$^{204}$" represent distinct word mentions and both nodes are linked to the word type "environmental".[1] For every edge in the graph, there exists an edge in the opposite direction (not shown in the figure). In this graph, the terms *disaster* and *catastrophe* are related due to the connecting path disaster $\longrightarrow$ disaster$^3$ $\xrightarrow{amod-inverse}$ environmental$^3$ $\longrightarrow$ environmental $\longrightarrow$ environmental$^{204}$ $\xrightarrow{amod}$ catastrophe$^{204}$ $\longrightarrow$ catastrophe .

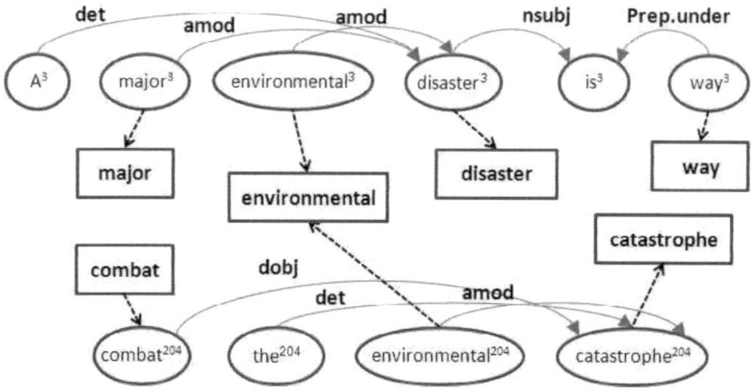


Figure 1: A joint graph of dependency structures

Given *a query*, which consists of a word of interest (e.g., 'disaster'), various graph-based similarity metrics can be used to assess inter-node relatedness, so that a list of nodes ranked by their similarity to the query is returned to the user. An advantage of graph-based similarity approaches is that they produce similarity scores that reflect structural infor-

[1] We will sometimes refer to *word types* as *terms*.

mation in the graph (Liben-Nowell and Kleinberg, 2003). Semantically similar terms are expected to share connectivity patterns with the query term in the graph, and thus appear at the top of the list.

Notably, different edge types, as well as the paths traversed, may have varying importance for different types of similarity sought. For example, in the parsed text domain, noun similarity and verb similarity are associated with different syntactic phenomena (Resnik and Diab, 2000). To this end, we consider a *path constrained graph walk* (PCW) algorithm, which allows one to learn meaningful paths given a small number of labeled examples and incorporates this information in assessing node relatedness in the graph (Minkov and Cohen, 2008). PCW have been successfully applied to the extraction of named entity coordinate terms, including city and person names, from graphs representing newswire text (Minkov and Cohen, 2008), where the specialized measures learned outperformed the state-of-the-art *dependency vectors* method (Padó and Lapata, 2007) for small- and medium-sized corpora.

In this work, we apply the path constrained graph walk method to the task of eliciting general word relatedness from parsed text, conducting a set of experiments on the task of synonym extraction. While the tasks of named entity extraction and synonym extraction from text have been treated separately in the literature, this work shows that both tasks can be addressed using the same general framework. Our results are encouraging: the PCW model yields superior results to the dependency vectors approach. Further, we show that learning specialized similarity measures per word type (nouns, verbs and adjectives) is preferable to applying a uniform model for all word types.

## 2 Path Constrained Graph Walks

PCW is a graph walk variant proposed recently that is intended to bias the random walk process to follow meaningful edge sequences (paths) (Minkov and Cohen, 2008). In this approach, rather than assume fixed (possibly, uniform) edge weight parameters $\Theta$ for the various edge types in the graph, the probability of following an edge of type $\ell$ from node $x$ is evaluated dynamically, based on the *history* of the walk up to $x$.

The PCW algorithm includes two components. First, it should provide estimates of edge weights conditioned on the history of a walk, based on training examples. Second, the random walk algorithm has to be modified to maintain historical information about the walk compactly.

In learning, a dataset of $N$ labelled example queries is provided. The labeling schema is binary, where a set of nodes considered as relevant answers to an example query $e_i$, denoted as $R_i$, is specified, and graph nodes that are not explicitly included in $R_i$ are assumed irrelevant to $e_i$. As a starting point, an initial graph walk is applied to generate a ranked list of graph nodes $l_i$ for every example query $e_i$. A path-tree $T$ is then constructed that includes all of the acyclic paths up to length $k$ leading to the top $M^+$ correct and $M^-$ incorrect nodes in each of the retrieved lists $l_i$. Every path $p$ is associated with a maximum likelihood probability estimate $Pr(p)$ of reaching a correct node based on the number of times the path was observed in the set of correct and incorrect target nodes. These path probabilities are propagated backwards in the path tree to reflect the probability of reaching a correct node, given an outgoing edge type and partial history of the walk.

Given a new query, a constrained graph walk variant is applied that adheres both to the topology of the graph $G$ and the path tree $T$. In addition to tracking the graph node that the random walker is at, PCW maintains pointers to the nodes of the path tree that represent the walk histories in reaching that graph node. In order to reduce working memory requirements, one may prune paths that are associated with low probability of reaching a correct node. This often leads to gains in accuracy.

## 3 Synonym Extraction

We learn general word semantic similarity measures from a graph that represents a corpus of parsed text (Figure 1). In particular, we will focus on evaluating word synonymy, learning specialized models for different word types. In the experiments, we mainly compare PCW against the dependency vectors model (DV), due to Padó and Lapata (2007). In the latter approach, a word $w_i$ is represented as a vector of weighted scores, which reflect co-occurrence frequency with words $w_j$, as well as properties of the dependency paths that connect the word $w_i$ to word $w_j$. In particular, higher weight is assigned to connecting paths that include grammatically salient relations, based on the *obliqueness* weighting hierarchy (Keenan and Comrie, 1977). For example, co-occurrence of word $w_i$ with word $w_j$ over a path that includes the salient *subject* relation receives higher credit than co-occurrences over a non-salient relation such as preposition. In addition, Padó and Lapata suggest to consider only a subset of the paths observed that are linguistically meaningful. While the two methods incorporate similar intuitions, PCW learns meaningful paths that connect the query and target terms from examples, whereas DV involves manual choices that are task-independent.

### 3.1 Dataset

To allow effective learning, we constructed a dataset that represents strict word synonymy relations for multiple word types. The dataset consists of 68 examples, where each example query consists of a single term of interest, with its synonym defined as a single correct answer. The dataset includes noun synonym pairs (22 examples), adjectives (24) and verbs (22). Example synonym pairs are shown in Table 1. A corpus of parsed text was constructed using the British National Corpus (Burnard, 1995). The full BNC corpus is a 100-million word collection of samples of written and spoken contemporary British English texts. We extracted relevant sentences, which contained the synonymous words, from the BNC corpus. (The number of extracted sentences was limited to 2,000 per word.) For infrequent words, we extracted additional example sentences from Associated Press (AP) articles included in the AQUAINT corpus (Bilotti et al., 2007). (Sentence count was complemented to 300 per word, where applicable.) The constructed corpus, BNC+AP, includes 1.3 million words overall. This corpus was parsed using the Stanford dependency parser (de Marneffe et al., 2006).[2]. The parsed corpus corresponds to a graph that includes about 0.5M nodes and 1.7M edges.

[2]http://nlp.stanford.edu/software/lex-parser.shtml

| | |
|---|---|
| *Nouns* | movie : film<br>murderer : assassin |
| *Verbs* | answered : replied<br>enquire : investigate |
| *Adjectives* | contemporary : modern<br>infrequent : rare |

Table 1: Example word synonym pairs: the left words are used as the query terms.

### 3.2 Experiments

Given a query like $\{term=\text{“}movie\text{”}\}$, we would like to get synonymous words, such as *film*, to appear at the top of the retrieved list. In our experimental setting, we assume that the word type of the query term is known. Rather than rank all words (terms) in response to a query, we use available (noisy) part of speech information to narrow down the search to the terms of the same type as the query term, e.g. for the query “film” we retrieve nodes of type $\tau = noun$.

We applied the PCW method to learn separate models for noun, verb and adjective queries. The path trees were constructed using the paths leading to the node known to be a correct answer, as well as to the otherwise irrelevant top-ranked 10 terms. We required the paths considered by PCW to include exactly 6 segments (edges). Such paths represent distributional similarity phenomena, allowing a direct comparison against the DV method. In conducting the constrained walk, we applied a threshold of 0.5 to truncate paths associated with lower probability of reaching a relevant response, following on previous work (Minkov and Cohen, 2008). We implemented DV using code made available by its authors,[3] where we converted the syntactic patterns specified to Stanford dependency parser conventions. The parameters of the DV method were set to *medium* context and *oblique* edge weighting scheme, which were found to perform best (Padó and Lapata, 2007). In applying a vector-space based method, a similarity score needs to be computed between *every* candidate from the corpus and the query term to construct a ranked list. In practice, we used the union of the top 300 words retrieved by PCW as candidate terms for DV.

We evaluate the following variants of DV: hav-

[3]http://www.coli.uni-saarland.de/~pado/dv.html

| | Nouns | Verbs | Adjs | All |
|---|---|---|---|---|
| **CO-Lin** | 0.34 | 0.37 | 0.37 | 0.37 |
| **DV-Cos** | 0.24 | 0.36 | 0.26 | 0.29 |
| **DV-Lin** | 0.45 | 0.49 | 0.54 | 0.50 |
| **PCW** | 0.47 | 0.55 | 0.47 | 0.49 |
| **PCW-P** | **0.53** | **0.68** | **0.55** | **0.59** |
| **PCW-P-U** | 0.49 | 0.65 | 0.50 | 0.54 |

Table 2: 5-fold cross validation results: MAP

ing inter-word similarity computed using Lin's measure (Lin, 1998) (DV-Lin), or using cosine similarity (DV-Cos). In addition, we consider a non-syntactic variant, where a word's vector consists of its co-occurrence counts with other terms (using a window of two words); that is, ignoring the dependency structure (CO-Lin).

Finally, in addition to the PCW model described above (PCW), we evaluate the PCW approach in settings where random, noisy, edges have been eliminated from the underlying graph. Specifically, dependency links in the graph may be associated with pointwise mutual information (PMI) scores of the linked word mention pairs (Manning and Schütze, 1999); edges with low scores are assumed to represent word co-occurrences of low significance, and so are removed. We empirically set the PMI score threshold to 2.0, using cross validation (PCW-P).[4] In addition to the specialized PCW models, we also learned a uniform model over all word types in these settings; that is, this model is trained using the union of all training examples, being learned and tested using a mixture of queries of all types (PCW-P-U).

### 3.3 Results

Table 2 gives the results of 5-fold cross-validation experiments in terms of mean average precision (MAP). Since there is a single correct answer per query, these results correspond to the mean reciprocal rank (MRR).[5] As shown, the dependency vectors model applied using Lin similarity (DV-Lin) performs best among the vector-based models. The improvement achieved due to edge weighting compared with the co-occurrence model (CO-Lin) is large, demonstrating that syntactic structure is very informative for modeling word semantics (Padó and Lapata, 2007). Interestingly, the impact of applying the Lin similarity measure versus cosine (DV-Cos) is even more profound. Unlike the cosine measure, Lin's metric was designed for the task of evaluating word similarity from corpus statistics; it is based on the mutual information measure, and allows one to downweight random word co-occurrences.

Among the PCW variants, the specialized PCW models achieve performance that is comparable to the state-of-the-art DV measure (DV-Lin). Further, removing noisy word co-occurrences from the graph (PCW-P) leads to further improvements, yielding the best results over all word types. Finally, the graph walk model that was trained uniformly for all word types (PCW-P-U) outperforms DV-Lin, showing the advantage of *learning* meaningful paths. Notably, the uniformly trained model is inferior to PCW trained separately per word type in the same settings (PCW-P). This suggests that learning *specialized* word similarity metrics is beneficial.

## 4 Discussion

We applied a path constrained graph walk variant to the task of extracting word synonyms from parsed text. In the past, this graph walk method has been shown to perform well on a related task, of extracting named entity coordinate terms from text. While the two tasks are typically treated distinctly, we have shown that they can be addressed using the same framework. Our results on a medium-sized corpus were shown to exceed the performance of *dependency vectors*, a syntactic state-of-the-art vector-space method. Compared to DV, the graph walk approach considers higher-level information about the connecting paths between word pairs, and are adaptive to the task at hand. In particular, we showed that learning specialized graph walk models for different word types is advantageous. The described framework can be applied towards learning other flavors of specialized word relatedness models (e.g., hypernymy). Future research directions include learning word similarity measures from graphs that integrate corpus statistics with word ontologies, as well as improved scalability (Lao and Cohen, 2010).

[4]Eliminating low PMI co-occurrences has been shown to be beneficial in modeling lexical selectional preferences recently, using a similar threshold value (Thater et al., 2010).

[5]The query's word inflections and words that are semantically related but not synonymous were discarded from the ranked list manually for evaluation purposes.

## References

Regina Barzilay and Michael Elhadad. 1999. *Text summarizations with lexical chains, in Inderjeet Mani and Mark Maybury, editors, Advances in Automatic Text Summarization*. MIT.

Matthew W. Bilotti, Paul Ogilvie, Jamie Callan, and Eric Nyberg. 2007. Structured retrieval for question answering. In *SIGIR*.

Lou Burnard. 1995. *Users Guide for the British National Corpus*. British National Corpus Consortium, Oxford University Computing Service, Oxford, UK.

Marie-Catherine de Marneffe, Bill MacCartney, and Christopher D. Manning. 2006. Generating typed dependency parses from phrase structure parses. In *LREC*.

Zellig Harria. 1968. *Mathematical Structures of Language*. Wiley, New York.

Thad Hughes and Daniel Ramage. 2007. Lexical semantic relatedness with random graph walks. In *EMNLP*.

Edward Keenan and Bernard Comrie. 1977. Noun phrase accessibility and universal grammar. *Linguistic Inquiry*, 8.

Ni Lao and William W. Cohen. 2010. Fast query execution for retrieval models based on path constrained random walks. In *KDD*.

Liben-Nowell and J. Kleinberg. 2003. The link prediction problem for social networks. In *CIKM*.

Dekang Lin and Patrick Pantel. 2001. Discovery of inference rules for question answering. *Natural Language Engineering*, 7(4).

Dekang Lin. 1998. Automatic retrieval and clustering of similar words. In *COLING-ACL*.

Chris Manning and Hinrich Schütze. 1999. *Foundations of Statistical Natural Language Processing*. MIT Press.

Einat Minkov and William W. Cohen. 2008. Learning graph walk based similarity measures for parsed text. In *EMNLP*.

Shachar Mirkin, Ido Dagan, and Maayan Geffet. 2006. Integrating pattern-based and distributional similarity methods for lexical entailment acquisition. In *ACL*.

Sebastian Padó and Mirella Lapata. 2007. Dependency-based construction of semantic space models. *Computational Linguistics*, 33(2).

Philip Resnik and Mona Diab. 2000. Measuring verb similarity. In *Proceedings of the Annual Meeting of the Cognitive Science Society*.

Stefan Thater, Hagen F́urstenau, and Manfred Pinkal. 2010. Contextualizing semantic representations using syntactically enriched vector models. In *ACL*.

# Semantic Relatedness for Biomedical Word Sense Disambiguation

**Kiem-Hieu Nguyen and Cheol-Young Ock**
School of Electrical Engineering
University of Ulsan
93, Daehakro, Nam-gu, Ulsan 680-749, Korea
{hieunk,okcy}@mail.ulsan.ac.kr

## Abstract

This paper presents a graph-based method for all-word word sense disambiguation of biomedical texts using semantic relatedness as edge weight. Semantic relatedness is derived from a term-topic co-occurrence matrix. The sense inventory is generated by the MetaMap program. Word sense disambiguation is performed on a disambiguation graph via a vertex centrality measure. The proposed method achieves competitive performance on a benchmark dataset.

## 1 Introduction

Word Sense Disambiguation (WSD) has been an open problem in Computational Linguistics (Navigli, 2009). It aims at identifying the correct meaning of an ambiguous word in a given context, e.g., 'adjustment' could refer to *individual adjustment* or *adjustment action* in "*marital adjustment*" and "*dietary adjustment*", respectively.

Supervised methods outperform unsupervised and knowledge-based methods (McInnes, 2009; Nguyen and Ock, 2010). However, they require expensive manual annotations and only the words of which training data are available could be disambiguated. On the other hand, knowledge-based and unsupervised methods overcome the two shortcomings by using knowledge sources or untagged raw texts (McInnes, 2008; Agirre et al., 2010; Ponzetto and Navigli, 2010).

Among knowledge-based methods, the graph-based method using semantic relatedness achieves state-of-the-art performance (Sinha and Mihalcea, 2007; Nguyen and Ock, 2011). This work aims at applying the method to the biomedical domain.

| Concept | Semantic Type |
|---|---|
| *Individual adjustment* | *Individual Behavior* |
| *Adjustment action* | *Functional Concept* |
| *Psychological adjustment* | *Mental Process* |

Table 1: The UMLS concepts and appropriate Semantic Types of the term 'adjustment'.

This paper proposes calculating semantic relatedness between Semantic Types based on the Semantic Type Indexing (Humphrey et al., 2006) algorithm. WSD is then perform via a state-of-the-art graph-based method (Sinha and Mihalcea, 2007). The proposed method achieves competitive performance on a benchmark dataset.

The paper is organized as follows: Section 2 presents the graph-based WSD method; Section 3 describes the calculation of semantic relatedness; Experimental results are showed in Section 4; The paper ends with conclusions in Section 5.

## 2 The WSD Method

Sense inventory is essential for WSD. In the biomedical domain, the MetaMap program (Aronson, 2001) has been used to generate concept candidates in the Unified Medical Language System (Bodenreider, 2004) (UMLS) for ambiguous terms.

The concepts in the UMLS are assigned to predefined topics called Semantic Types (ST) (Table 1). Hence, STs could be efficiently used for disambiguation of biomedical terms (Humphrey et al., 2006). For instance, if the term 'adjustment' is mapped to the ST *Mental Process* then it is disambiguated as *psychological adjustment*.

The WSD method used in this work is derived from Sinha and Mihalcea (2007) with an additional postprocessing step (Humphrey et al., 2006). The method consists of three steps:

- A disambiguation graph is generated for each context. The vertices are STs. The edge weight is semantic relatedness between STs (Section 3).
- Each ambiguous term is mapped to the ST with the highest rank based on vertex centrality.
- The term is disambiguated as the appropriate concept of the selected ST.

On the one hand, *i)* the method achieves state-of-the-art performance for WSD on general texts using WordNet (Miller, 1995) as sense inventory and the source to calculate semantic relatedness (Sinha and Mihalcea, 2007; Nguyen and Ock, 2011). By far, semantic relatedness between biomedical concepts has been studied on the UMLS meta-thesaurus (Pedersen et al., 2007) but there has been no work on applying semantic relatedness (particularly between STs) to biomedical WSD. On the other hand, *ii)* the method is effective in terms of implementation, comprehension, and computational complexity.

## 2.1 Disambiguation Graph

The **Algorithm 1** generates an undirected fully connected disambiguation graph for a context $C = \{w_0, w_1, \cdots, w_n\}$. The dictionary $D$ maps from an ambiguous term $w_i$ to its ST candidates $D(w_i)$. $D$ is generated by MetaMap. Given a term $w_i$, MetaMap generates a list of its UMLS concept candidates. In UMLS, each concept is, in turn, assigned to one or several STs. From that, we can create a list of ST candidates for $w_i$. The resulted disambiguation graph $G$ contains vertices as STs and weight edge as semantic relatedness between STs.

From line 1 to line 8, the algorithm generates the vertices of $G$ from the dictionary. From line 9 to line 15, the algorithm calculates the edge weight as semantic relatedness between STs (3).

**Algorithm 1** Disambiguation graph creation

**Input:** Context $\{w_0, w_1, \cdots, w_n\}$.
**Input:** Dictionary $D$
**Output:** Disambiguation graph $G = (V, E)$
1: $V \leftarrow \phi$ # Initialize graph vertices.
2: **for all** $w_i \in w$ **do**
3:   **for all** $ST_i \in D(w_i)$ **do**
4:     **if** $ST_i \notin V$ **then**
5:       $V \leftarrow V \cup \{ST_i\}$
6:     **end if**
7:   **end for**
8: **end for**
9: $E \leftarrow \phi$ # Initialize the edges of the graph.
10: **for all** $ST_i \in V$ **do**
11:   **for all** $ST_j \in V \setminus \{\{ST_i\} \cup D^{-1}(ST_i)\}$ **do**
12:     $e_{ST_i,ST_j} \leftarrow sr(ST_i, ST_j)$
13:     $E \leftarrow E \cap \{e_{ST_i,ST_j}\}$
14:   **end for**
15: **end for**
16: **return** $G = (V, E)$

## 2.2 Disambiguation based on Vertex Centrality

Given the disambiguation graph $G$, the rank of a vertex $ST_i$ is defined as its weighted node-degree (shortly as *degree*):

$$degree(ST_i) = \sum_{ST_j \in V, e_{ST_i,ST_j} \in E} e_{ST_i,ST_j}, \qquad (1)$$

For each ambiguous term $w_i$, the ST with the highest rank is selected among its ST candidates:

$$\underset{ST_k \in D(w_i)}{argmax}\ degree(ST_k) \qquad (2)$$

While there are alternative vertex centrality measures such as *betweenness*, *closeness*, and *eigenvector centrality*, empirical evidences show that *degree* achieves state-of-the-art performance on several benchmark datasets (Sinha and Mihalcea, 2007; Ponzetto and Navigli, 2010; Nguyen and Ock, 2011).

Given a sentence "*Clinically, these four patients had mild symptoms which improved with dietary adjustment*", the terms not existing in the sense inventory are ignored, the rest are mapped to ST candidates as ('four': *Quantitative Concept*, 'patients': *Patient or Disabled Group*; 'mild': *Qualitative Concept*; 'symptoms': *Functional Concept*, *Sign or*

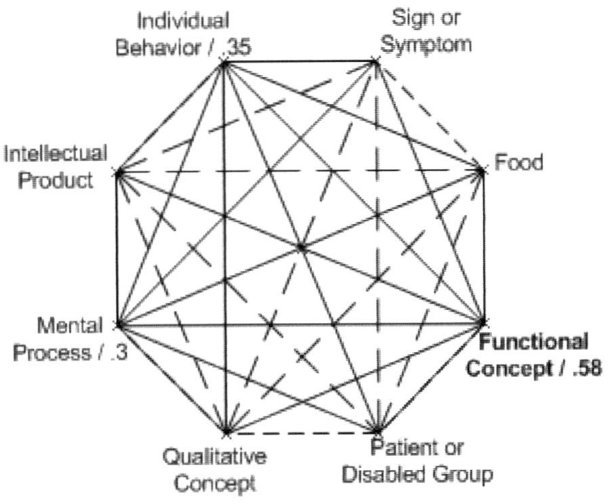


Figure 1: The disambiguation graph for "*Clinically, these four patients had mild symptoms which improved with dietary adjustment*". The edges containing the ST candidates of 'adjustment' are solid lines, the rest are dot lines.

*Symptom*; 'improved': *Qualitative Concept, Intellectual Product*; 'dietary': *Food*; 'adjustment': *Individual Behavior, Functional Concept, Mental Process*). The disambiguation graph hence contains eight STs (Fig. 1).

If we want to disambiguate, for instance, 'adjustment', we could compare the degree of its ST candidates. As seen in Fig. 1, *Functional Concept* is the highest rank ST. Consequently, 'adjustment' is disambiguated as *adjustment action* (not *individual adjustment* or *psychological adjustment*).

## 3 Semantic Relatedness between STs

### 3.1 Motivations

Pedersen et al. (2007) show that there is no general-purpose measure among the six state-of-the-art semantic relatedness measures calculated based on the UMLS ontology and medical corpora. For instance, the corpus-based measure is close to physician judgments while the path-based and information content based measures are close to medical coders judgments. This is one of the main obstacles that prevent the use of semantic relatedness between concepts for biomedical WSD.

In another direction, Humphrey et al. (2006) induce a term-ST matrix from medical corpora. The WSD method proposed in that work is similar to the *Lesk* algorithm (Lesk, 1986) where each ST *profile* is compared with the context using the term-ST matrix to select the highest rank ST. Nguyen and Ock (2011) show that using the same *synset profiles* in WordNet, the Lesk-based method achieves higher *precision* but lower *recall* than the semantic relatedness-based method.

### 3.2 The Proposed Measure

Semantic relatedness between STs is calculated from a term-ST matrix $A_{m,n}$ proposed in the Semantic Type Indexing algorithm (Humphrey et al., 2006) where $m$ is the number of STs and $n$ is the size of vocabulary. $A_{i,j}$ is the normalized frequency that the $i^{th}$ ST and the $j^{th}$ term co-occur. Hence, each row of the matrix is an ST *profile* that can be used to calculate context-sensitive semantic relatedness between STs as follows:

- Given a set of terms $\{w_0, w_1, w_2, ..., w_n\}$ in a context $C$ and the term-ST matrix $A$.
- The static vector of the $i^{th}$ ST is $A_i$, the $i^{th}$ row of $A$. $A(i)$ contains all the terms in the vocabulary. $A_i(C)$ is generated from $A_i$ by assigning *zero* to all the terms not in $C$ .
- The context-sensitive semantic relatedness of the $i^{th}$ and $j^{th}$ STs is defined as the dot product of the two context-sensitive vectors:

$$sr(ST_i, ST_j) = A_i(C) \cdot A_j(C) \quad (3)$$

## 4 Experiments

### 4.1 Test Dataset

The NLM-WSD dataset contains 5,000 contexts of 50 frequent ambiguous biomedical terms from the paper abstracts of the 1998 MEDILINE database (Weeber et al., 2001). Each ambiguous term has 100 contexts including the surrounding sentence, paper title and abstract. The average number of senses per term is 3.28.

### 4.2 Experimental Setups

The MetaMap program was used to generate ST candidates of ambiguous terms.

The *most frequent sense* (*MFS*) heuristic was used as the baseline system: For each ambiguous term,

| System | A | P | R | F |
|---|---|---|---|---|
| *SR* | 93.2 | **74.8** | **69.7** | **72.2** |
| *Static-SR* | 95.0 | 66.2 | 62.9 | 64.5 |
| *STI* | 93.2 | 74.1 | 69.0 | 71.5 |
| *PPR* | **100.0** | 68.1 | 68.1 | 68.1 |
| *MFS* | 100.0 | 85.5 | 85.5 | 85.5 |

Table 2: Experimental results on the NLM-WSD dataset.

the most frequent concept calculated based on the NLM-WSD dataset is simply selected.

The experimental results were compared using *attempted*, *precision*, *recall* and *F-measure* (A, P, R, and F, respectively).

### 4.3 Experimental Results

The proposed method, namely *SR*, was compared with three knowledge-based systems:

- *Static-SR*: The system uses static ST vectors, i.e., $A_i$, instead of context-sensitive ST vectors, i.e., $A_i(C)$ as described in Section 3.

- *STI*[1] (Humphrey et al., 2006): For a context, the rank of an ST candidate is the average ranks across all words in the context, e.g., for the context *Clinically, these four patients had mild symptoms which improved with dietary adjustment*, the rank of *Functional Concept* is [ .5314 ('symptoms') + .4714 ('adjustment') + .7149 ('patients') + .1804 ('dietary') + .7226 ('mild') + .7282 ('improved') + .7457 ('four') ] / 7 = .5849.

- *PPR*[2] (Agirre et al., 2010): The system uses the UMLS metathesaurus as a lexical knowledge graph and executes the Personalized PageRank, a state-of-the-art graph-based method, on the graph (Agirre and Soroa, 2009).

The performance of the *MFS* baseline is remarkably high, i.e., 85.5% of *F-measure* (Table 2). This shows that the sense distribution in the biomedical domain is highly skewed. Hence, this simple supervised heuristic outperformed all the investigated knowledge-based systems.

[1]Available as a component of the MetaMap program.

[2]http://ixa2.si.ehu.es/ukb

Because *STI* and *SR* performed WSD via the disambiguation of STs, the two systems failed when the ST with the highest rank was assigned to at least two concepts. For instance, given the term 'cold', if *Disease or Syndrome* scores the highest rank, the two systems cannot decide whether *common cold* or *chronic obstructive airway disease* is the correct concept. Hence, the *attempted* status of *SR* and *STI* didn't reach 100%.

*SR* was remarkably superior to *Static-SR* which empirically supports the context-sensitive ST vectors over static ones. Overall, *SR* and *STI* achieved the best performance.

## 5 Conclusions

In our experiments, the ST *profiles* were induced from the term-ST co-occurrence matrix. On the other hand, semantic relations and textual definitions in WordNet are useful for word sense disambiguation (Ponzetto and Navigli, 2010; Nguyen and Ock, 2011). Hence, the semantic relations between STs and the textual definitions of ST in the Unified Medical Language System could be potential resources for the disambiguation of biomedical texts.

The paper presents a graph-based method to biomedical word sense disambiguation using semantic relatedness between pre-defined biomedical topics. The proposed method achieves competitive performance on the NLM-WSD dataset. Because the achieved performance is significantly inferior to the performance of the most frequent sense heuristic, there is still more ground for improvement.

## Acknowledgments

This work is partially supported by a scholarship of the Korean Ministry of Information and Communication. The first author receives a tuition fellowship of PhD course from the University of Ulsan, Korea. The authors would like to thank the United States National Library of Medicine for providing the NLM-WSD dataset and the MetaMap program, and the anonymous reviewers for their suggestions.

## References

E. Agirre and A. Soroa. 2009. Personalizing PageRank for Word Sense Disambiguation. In *Proceedings of the*

*12th Conference of the European Chapter of the ACL (EACL 2009)*, pages 33–41, Athens, Greece, March. Association for Computational Linguistics.

E. Agirre, A. Soroa, and M. Stevenson. 2010. Graph-based word sense disambiguation of biomedical documents. *Bioinformatics*, 26:2889–2896, November.

AR Aronson. 2001. Effective mapping of biomedical text to the UMLS metathesaurus: the MetaMap program. *Proceedings / AMIA ... Annual Symposium. AMIA Symposium*, pages 17–21.

O. Bodenreider. 2004. The unified medical language system (UMLS): integrating biomedical terminology. *Nucleic Acids Research*, 32(Database issue):D267–D270, January. PMID: 14681409 PMCID: 308795.

S. M. Humphrey, W. J. Rogers, H. Kilicoglu, D. Demner-Fushman, and T. C. Rindflesch. 2006. Word sense disambiguation by selecting the best semantic type based on journal descriptor indexing: Preliminary experiment. *J. Am. Soc. Inf. Sci. Technol.*, 57:96–113, January.

Michael Lesk. 1986. Automatic sense disambiguation using machine readable dictionaries: how to tell a pine cone from an ice cream cone. In *Proceedings of the 5th annual international conference on Systems documentation*, SIGDOC '86, pages 24–26, New York, NY, USA. ACM.

B. T. McInnes. 2008. An unsupervised vector approach to biomedical term disambiguation: integrating umls and medline. In *Proceedings of the 46th Annual Meeting of the Association for Computational Linguistics on Human Language Technologies: Student Research Workshop*, HLT-SRWS '08, pages 49–54, Stroudsburg, PA, USA. Association for Computational Linguistics.

B. T. McInnes. 2009. Supervised and knowledge-based methods for disambiguating terms in biomedical text using the umls and metamap.

G. A. Miller. 1995. Wordnet: a lexical database for english. *Commun. ACM*, 38:39–41, November.

R. Navigli. 2009. Word sense disambiguation: A survey. *ACM Comput. Surv.*, 41:10:1–10:69, February.

K. H. Nguyen and Ch. Y. Ock. 2010. Margin perceptron for word sense disambiguation. In *Proceedings of the 2010 Symposium on Information and Communication Technology*, SoICT '10, pages 64–70, New York, NY, USA. ACM.

K. H. Nguyen and Ch. Y. Ock. 2011. Word sense disambiguation as a traveling salesman problem. *Artificial Intelligence Review*, December.

T. Pedersen, S. V. S. Pakhomov, S. Patwardhan, and Ch. G. Chute. 2007. Measures of semantic similarity and relatedness in the biomedical domain. *J. of Biomedical Informatics*, 40:288–299, June.

S. P. Ponzetto and R. Navigli. 2010. Knowledge-rich word sense disambiguation rivaling supervised systems. In *Proceedings of the 48th Annual Meeting of the Association for Computational Linguistics*, ACL '10, pages 1522–1531, Stroudsburg, PA, USA. Association for Computational Linguistics.

R. Sinha and R. Mihalcea. 2007. Unsupervised Graph-basedWord Sense Disambiguation Using Measures of Word Semantic Similarity. In *Proceedings of the International Conference on Semantic Computing*, pages 363–369, Washington, DC, USA. IEEE Computer Society.

M. Weeber, J. G. Mork, and A. R. Aronson. 2001. Developing a test collection for biomedical word sense disambiguation. *Proceedings / AMIA ... Annual Symposium. AMIA Symposium*, pages 746–750. PMID: 11825285.

# Identifying Untyped Relation Mentions in a Corpus given an Ontology

**Gabor Melli**
VigLink Inc.
539 Bryant St. #400
San Francisco, CA, USA
gabor@viglink.com

**Abstract**

In this paper we present the $SDOI_{rmi}$ text graph-based semi-supervised algorithm for the task for relation mention identification when the underlying concept mentions have already been identified and linked to an ontology. To overcome the lack of annotated data, we propose a labelling heuristic based on information extracted from the ontology. We evaluated the algorithm on the kdd09cma1 dataset using a leave-one-document-out framework and demonstrated an increase in F1 in performance over a co-occurrence based AllTrue baseline algorithm. An extrinsic evaluation of the predictions suggests a worthwhile precision on the more confidently predicted additions to the ontology.

## 1 Introduction

The growing availability of text documents and of ontologies will significantly increase in value once these two resources become deeply interlinked such that all of the concepts and relationships mentioned in each document link to their formal definitions. This type of semantic information can be used, for example, to aid information retrieval, textual entailment, text summarization, and ontology engineering (Staab & Studer, 2009; Buitelaar et al, 2009). An obstacle to this vision of semantically grounded documents however is the significant amount of effort required of domain experts to semantically annotate the text (Erdmann et al, 2000; Uren et al, 2006). Some automation of the annotation task is a precondition to the envisioned future of deeply interlinked information. Fortunately, the task of linking concept mentions to their referent in an ontology has matured (Milne & Witten, 2008; Melli & Ester, 2010). Far less progress has been made on the task of linking of relation mentions to the referent relation in a knowledge base. In part, we believe, this is because current approaches attempt to both identify mentions of relations between two or more concepts and to classify the type of the relation, such as one of: IsA(); HeadquarteredIn(); SubcecullarLocalization(), and ComposerOf()

In this paper, we present a weakly-supervised algorithm for the task of <u>r</u>elation <u>m</u>ention <u>i</u>dentification, SDOI[1] $_{RMI}$. Given a corpus of documents whose concept mentions have been identified and linked to an ontology, the algorithm trains a binary classification model that predicts the relations mentioned within a document that should be (and possibly already are) in an ontology. To overcome the lack of explicit annotation of relation mentions, we propose the use of a data labelling heuristic that assigns a TRUE or FALSE label if the candidate mention refers to a link that exists or does not exist in the ontology. $SDOI_{RMI}$.is related to proposals by (Riedel et al, 2010) and (Mintz et al, 2009) except that their proposal attempt to both identify and to classify relation mentions. By only tackling the first (identification) portion of the task our

[1] **SDOI** is for **S**upervised **D**ocument to **O**ntology **I**nterlinking

algorithm can identify relation mentions of types that are not yet present (or are poorly represented) in the ontology. An extrinsic evaluation of the usability of identified relation mentions to update an ontology provides evidence that $SDOI_{RMI}$'s performance levels can contribute to a real-world setting.

Our envisioned real-world application is to assist a knowledge engineer to process a new set of documents by receiving a ranked list of candidate relation mentions not yet in the ontology. With such a list, the knowledge engineer could dedicate more attention to comprehending the meaning of the passages that (very likely) contain high-quality relation mention candidates.

The paper is structured as follows: we first define our proposed algorithm: **$SDOI_{rmi}$**,, and conclude with an empirical analysis of its performance.

## 2 Algorithm Overview

For the task of relation mention identification, we propose a semi-supervised algorithm inspired by the **TeGRR** text graph-based relation recognition algorithm proposed in (Melli & al, 2007). The algorithm first applies a labelling heuristic to unlabeled candidate relation mentions, and then trains a binary classification model. We were motivated to follow this approach used by **TeGRR** for the following reasons:

1) It is based on relation recognition approaches, such as (Jiang & Zhai, 2007), that achieve state-of-the-art performance (e.g. on benchmark tasks such as ACE[2]).
2) It is designed to recognize relation mentions that span beyond a single sentence (by the use of a text graph representation)
3) It exposes an extensible feature space (that can be extended with information drawn from our task's ontology).
4) It provides a natural path for the future support of tasks with labelled training data – possibly even labelled with the actual relation type.

One of the distinctive aspects of **TeGRR** is its representation of a document into a graph-based representation, where each concept mention or token in the text is mapped to an 'external' node in a graph, and which represents other syntactic and structural features of the text as internal nodes and edges between nodes. In Section 3 we define the text graph representation and its effect on the algorithm definition.

Given a document's text-graph, we can proceed to define a feature space for each relation mention candidate. Table 1 illustrates the structure of the training data and its feature space that we propose for $SDOI_{rmi}$. We divide the feature space into three information sources. An initial feature source is based on the shortest path between the concepts mentions, all of which have been proposed for TeGRR in (Melli & al, 2007). We also propose to inherit the concept mention linking features defined in (Melli & al, 2010) for each of the two concept mentions associated to a relation mention candidate. Finally, we also propose features that draw on information from the ontology.

| Relation Mention | | | TeGRR Text-Graph based | Concept Mention (CM) Linking based | | Ontology based | label |
|---|---|---|---|---|---|---|---|
| $doc_d$ | $m_i$ | $m_j$ | | $CM_a$ | $CM_b$ | | |
| | | | | | | | T |
| | | | Feature Space | | | | F |
| | | | | | | | ... |

**Table 1 – A high-level representation of training examples of a document's unique concept mention pairs (relation mention candidates). The label assignment procedure and the feature definitions are presented in the two coming subsections.**

### 2.1 Label Assignment

Annotating relations in text is a time consuming process – more so than annotating entities. To overcome the lack of annotated relation mention data, we propose to use the ontology for the labeling decision. For each combination of concept mention pairs the heuristic automatically assign labels according to the following rule. If the concepts in the ontology associated with the relation mention share a direct internal link in the ontology in either direction then the training example is marked as true; otherwise it is labeled as False.

[2] ACE Relation Detection Recognition (RDR) task http://projects.ldc.upenn.edu/ace/annotation/

This approach to labeling is similar to the one used by relation mention recognition task such as (Melli & al, 2007). Our proposal in this paper however extends this automatic labeling approach for False example labeling to also automatically label true relation mentions. This approach is more likely to lead to erroneously mislabeled candidates. In many cases, the passages associated with a candidate relation mention that happens to refer to directly linked concepts in the ontology do not substantiate a direct semantic relation. In these cases, after reading the passage, an expert would instead conclude that a direct relation is not implied by the passage and would label the candidate relation mention as False. Alternatively, the heuristic would label some relation mention candidates as False simply because the relation did not yet exist in the ontology; while, upon manual inspection of the passage, the annotator would label the relation as a True candidate.

Despite this appreciation of noise in the generated labels, we hypothesize that this heuristic labeling approach provides a sufficient signal for the supervised classification algorithm to detect many direct relation mentions with sufficient accuracy to be useful in some real-world tasks, such as ontological engineering.

## 3 Text Graph Representation

The **TeGRR** feature space is based on a graph representation of the document under consideration. The text graph representation is composed of the three types of edges: 1) Intra-sentential edges; 2) Sentence-to-sentence edges; and 3) Co-reference edges.

**Figure 1 - An illustration of $SDOI_{RMI}$'s text graph to create feature vectors. The highlighted nodes and path represent the information used for a specific candidate pair assessment.**

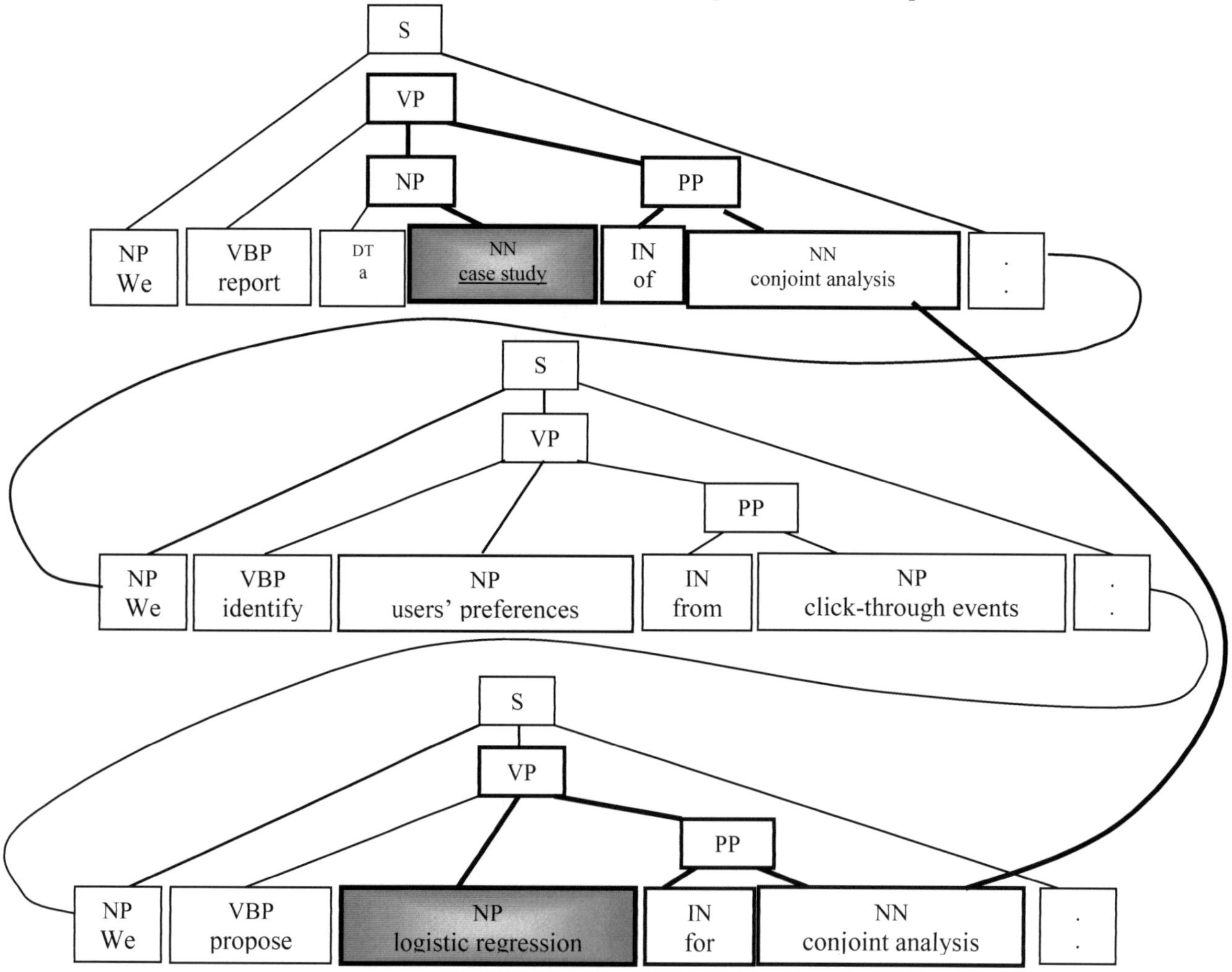

Intra-sentential edges in a text-graph represent edges between nodes associated with tokens from the same sentence. These edges can vary from being: word-to-word edges, shallow parsing edges, dependency parse tree edges, and phrase-structure parse tree edges. We propose the use the phrase-structure parse tree as the source of intrasentential edges for two reasons. The choice of this data source over the others is the analysis by (Jiang & Zhai, 2007) that suggests that the phrase-structure parse tree is the best single source of information for relation detection. Secondly, all other proposed intra-sentential edge types can be derived, or approximated, from phrase-structure parse trees by means of transformations.

A phrase-structure parse tree is composed of two types of nodes: leaf nodes and internal nodes. Leaf nodes (which map to our external nodes) are labelled with the text token (or concept mention), and with the part-of-speech role. Internal nodes contain the syntactic phrase-structure label.

The text graph in **Figure 1** contains 26 intrasentential edges connecting 12 internal nodes and 19 leaf nodes.

Edges in a text graph can also cross sentence boundaries. The first type of inter-sentential edge to be considered is the "sentence-to-sentence" edge that simply joins an end-of-sentence punctuation node with the first word of the sentence that follows. The intuition for this edge type is that a concept that is mentioned in one sentence can be in a semantic relation with a concept mention in the adjacent sentence, and that the likelihood of it being a relation increases as you reduce the number of sentences between the two entities. The text graph in **Figure 1** contains two sentence-to-sentence edges.

**Co-reference Edges**

The other source of inter-sentential edges to be considered, also taken from (Melli & al, 2007), are based on concept mentions in the same document that are linked to (co-refer to) the same concept in the ontology. For example if "*hidden-Markov models*" is mentioned in one sentence, "*HMMs*" is mentioned in a subsequent one, and the pronoun "*they*" is used to refer to the concept further on in the document, then coreference edges would exist between "*hidden-Markov models*" and "*HMMs*", and between "*HMM*" and "*they*" (via the Hidden Markov Models concept). The intuition for this edge type is that concept mentions in separate sentences but that are near some coreferent concept mention are more likely to be in a semantic relation than if that co-referent mention did not exist. The text graph in **Figure 1** contains a coreference edge between the mentions of to the Conjoint Analysis Algorithm that were identified by the concept mention identifier and disambiguator described in (Melli & Ester, 2010).

**Text-Graph Properties**

We describe properties of a text graph used to define $\mathbf{SDOI_{rmi}}$'s text-graph related features:

1) A text-graph is a connected graph: for every pair of nodes *n* and *v* there is a walk from *n* to *v*
2) A text-graph can be a cyclic graph, and such cycles must involve co-reference edges.
3) A text-graph has at least one shortest path between any two nodes, *n* and *v*, and the number of edges between them is their *distance*.
4) A concept mention $m_i$ is in a *p-shortest path* with concept mention $m_j$ if there are only *p*-1 other concept mentions in a shorter shortest-path relation with $m_i$. The value of *p* can be interpreted as the rank of the proximity between the two concept mentions, e.g. 1st nearest, 2nd nearest, etc. If two alternate mention pairs are in equal *p-shortest path relation* then both are True for the relation.
5) A path-enclosed subtree is the portion of the syntactic tree enclosed by the shortest-path between two leaf-nodes. This inner portion of a syntactic tree is predictive in relation extraction tasks (Jiang & Zhai, 2007).

## 4 Relation Mention Identification Features

We begin the definition of the feature space with the text-graph based features that we retain from (Melli & al, 2007). We then proceed to describe the ontology-based features, and conclude with the concept linking features inherited from the previous (concept linking) task.

## 4.1 Text-Graph based Features

This section describes the features that we directly inherit from TeGRR. We first describe the underlying text graph representation that is then used to define the associated features.

**Path-Enclosed Shortest Path Features**

From the path-enclosed shortest-path subgraph we identify all distinct subtrees with up to ***e*** edges as proposed in (Jiang & Zhai, 2007) to replicate the convolution-kernel approach of (Haussler, 1999). A feature is created for each possible *neighborhood* in the subgraph, where a neighborhood is defined by a subtrees with ***e*** edges, where ***e*** ranges from zero through to some upper limit on edges: $e$ □ $[0, e_{max}]$. We retain the ***e*** proposed in (Jiang & Zhai, 2007) of $e_{max}=2$. Subtree-based features associated to the subtrees of size zero ($e$=0) simply summarize the number of nodes of a certain content type in either the entire relation mention graph, or one of its pairings. For example, one feature would count the number of **NP** (Noun Phrase) nodes in the relation mention graph, while another feature would count the number of times that the word "*required*" is present. Subtree-based features associated to the subtrees of size $e$>0 represent the number of times that a subgraph with ***e*** edges appears within the subgraph. For example, one feature would count the number of times that the triple IN – PP – NP appears in the graph.

**Sentence Count:**

This feature informs the classifier about the number of sentences that intervene between concept mentions. For example, the number of intervening sentences between the "case study" and "logistic regression" mention in the relation mention in **Figure 1** is two (2) sentences. This information will help the classifier adjust its predictions based on the separation. Nearer mentions are more likely to be in a relation.

**Intervening Concept Mentions:**

This set of features informs the classifier about the number of concept mentions that intervene between two concept mention pairs. For example, in **Figure 1** "*conjoint analysis*" is counted as one intervening concept mention between "*case study*" and "*logistic regression*". This information will help the classifier adjust its predictions based on how many other concept mention candidates exist; the greater then number of intervening concept mentions the less likely that a semantic relation between the two concept mentions is being stated.

### 4.1.1 Concept Mention Linking-based Features

A second source of features that we propose is to include the pair of feature sets for each concept mention defined for concept mention linking (Melli & Ester, 2010). We concatenate the two feature vectors in the following order: the concept mention that appears first in the text, followed by the other concept mention. These features provide signals of the context of each mention, such as even simply what sentence it is locate on. In **Figure 1** for example, the "*case study*" concept mention is located on the first sentence and the closer a mention is to the first sentence may affect the importance of the mention.

## 4.2 Ontology-based Features

We further propose four features based on information from the ontology – that differ from the ones inherited from the concept-mention linking task. These four features capture information signals from their pairing in the ontology: Shared_Outlinks, Shared_Inlinks, Shortest_gt1-Edge_Distance, and TF-IDF_Concepts_Similarity.

**Shared_Outlinks Feature**

The Shared_Outlinks feature counts the number of shared concept outlinks. The intuition for this feature is that two concepts that reference many of the same other concepts in the ontology are more likely to be themselves in a direct relation.

**Shared_Inlinks Feature**

The Shared_Inlinks feature counts the number of shared concept inlinks. The intuition for this feature is that two concepts that are referenced by many of the same other concepts in the ontology are more likely to be themselves in a direct relation.

**Shortest1-Edge_Distance Feature**

The Shortest1-Edge_Distance feature reports the shortest distance (in the ontology) that is greater than one counts the number of edges that separate the two concepts. This feature is the one that introduces the risk of giving away the presence of a direct link between the two concepts in the candidate. An edge distance of one (1) versus any other edge distance would be a perfect predictor of the label. However, information about the distance of alternate paths can provide a signal that the two concepts should be (or are) linked.

**TF-IDF_Concepts_Similarity Feature**

The TF-IDF_Concepts_Similarity feature reports the tf-idf bag-of-words similarity between the two concept descriptions in the ontology. The intuition is similar to that of the "Shared Outlinks" feature: two concepts that reference many of the same words are more likely to be themselves in a relation. Unlike the "Shared Outlinks" feature however, this feature normalizes for very common and uncommon words.

**Corpus-based Features**

A final source of information for features that we propose is the training corpus itself. As with the corpus-based features for concept linking (Melli & Ester, 2010), the use of cross-validation for performance estimation requires that the document associated with the training record does not inform these features. For this feature, the count is on "other" documents.

### 4.3 Relation_Mention_Other_Doc_Count Feature

The Relation_Mention_Other_Doc_Count feature counts the number of other documents in the corpus that contain the pair of linked concept mentions. For example, if one other document contains the two linked concept mentions (and thus contains the same candidate relation mention) this feature is set to one (1).

## 5 Empirical Evaluation of Relation Mention Identification

In this section, we empirically evaluate the performance of the proposed relation-mention identification algorithm: $SDOI_{rmi}$. For this evaluation, we again used the SVMlight[3] package with its default parameter settings, as the underlying supervised classification algorithm. For the syntactic parse trees, we use Charniak's parser[4].

**Evaluation Setup**

Similar to evaluation of SDOI's two other component algorithms for concept mention identification and linking, we use a leave-one-document-out method on the kdd09cma1 corpus (Melli, 2010). For each unseen document, we predict which of its binary relation mention candidates (with linked concept mentions) already exist in the ontology. Those relations that do not exist in the ontology are proposed candidates for addition to the ontology.

A challenge associated with this task, as found in the concept-mention linking task, is the highly skewed distribution of the labels. In this case, we do not propose a filtering heuristic to change the training data. Instead, we propose an algorithmic change by tuning SVMlight's cost-factor parameter that multiplies the training error penalty for misclassification of positive examples. We set aside three documents to tune the parameter, and based on an analysis to optimize F1 we set the cost-factor to 8.

**Table 2** presents some of the key statistics for the kdd09cma1 from the perspective of relation mention candidates. The corpus contains 44,896 relation mention candidates. Of these, which quantifies the task's data skew, only 3.55% of the mention candidates are found in the ontology.

**Table 2 – Key statistics of the number of binary relation mentions in the kdd09cma1 corpus, per abstract and for entire corpus. The final row reports the total number of concept pairings where, at the document-level, pairs to the same two concepts are consolidated.**

| | Binary Relation Mention Candidates | Positive Candidates | Proportion |
|---|---|---|---|
| Minimum (per abstract) | 42.0 | 1.0 | 0.88% |
| Average (per abstract) | 322.1 | 11.5 | 3.86% |
| Maximum (per abstract) | 1,582.0 | 4.3 | 12.50% |
| Entire corpus | 44,896.0 | 1,593.0 | 3.55% |
| Entire corpus (only distinct relations) | 34,181.0 | 1,080.0 | 3.16% |

[3] http://svmlight.joachims.org/

[4] ftp://ftp.cs.brown.edu/pub/nlparser/

**Baseline Algorithm(s)**

The baseline algorithm that we compare $SDOI_{rml}$'s performance against on the relation-mention identification task is an unsupervised co-occurrence-based algorithm that predicts all permutations of linked concept mention pairs regardless of distance between them. This is the baseline algorithm compared against in (Melli & al, 2007, and Shi & al, 2007). We refer to this algorithm as **AllTrue**.

We also include as a baseline a version of $SDOI_{rml}$ with a restricted feature space that contains the features originally proposed for TeGRR.

**Intrinsic Performance Analysis**

**Table 3** presents the results of the leave-one out performance analysis. $SDOI_{rml}$ outperforms the baseline algorithm in terms of precision and F1. The proposed feature space for SDOI also outperforms the original feature space proposed for TeGRR.

| Algorithm | Feature Space | Precision | Recall | F1 |
|---|---|---|---|---|
| SDOI | All | 18.2% | 24.3% | 20.8% |
| | TeGRR | 7.7% | 41.8% | 13.0% |
| AllTrue | | 3.7% | 100.0% | 7.1% |

**Table 3 – Leave-one-out performance results on the relation mention identification task on the kdd09cma1 corpus (excluding the three tuning abstracts) by SDOI, SDOI with its feature space restricted to those originally proposed for TeGRR, and the AllTrue baseline.**

**Extrinsic Performance Analysis**

We analyze the performance on a real-world usage scenario where an ontology engineer receives the generated list of relation mention candidates predicted as True for being a direct link, which upon inspection of the ontology does not exist. We manually analyzed the top 40 predicted relation mention candidates proposed for insertion into the kddo1 ontology ranked on their likelihood score[5]. **Table 4** reports a snapshot of these relation candidates. Of the 40 candidates 31 (77.5%) were deemed candidates for insertion into the ontology[6]. Given the high proportion of relation candidates worthy of insertion, this result illustrates some benefit to the ontology engineer.

**Boostrapping Experiment**

In practice, a common method of applying self-labelled learning is to treat the labelling heuristic as a means to seed a bootstrapped process where subsequent rounds of labelling are based on the most confident predictions by the newly trained model (Chapelle & al, 2006). Generally, evaluations of this approach have assumed high-accuracy seed labels - either from a small manually curated training set, such as in (Agichtein & Gravano, 2000), or with high-accuracy labelling patterns, such as in (Yarowsky, 1995). Each iteration sacrifices some precision for additional recall performance. In our case a bootstrapped process does not begin with high precision to sacrifice, because of our labelling heuristic does not start with high-precision predictions.

| Score | Binary Relation | | Document |
|---|---|---|---|
| | Concept A | Concept B | |
| 20.873 | Computing System | Algorithm | doi:10.1145/1557019.1557112 |
| ... | ... | ... | ... |
| 15.975 | Computing System | Algorithm | doi:10.1145/1557019.1557144 |
| 23.584 | Conditional Probability | Marginal Probabilty | doi:10.1145/1557019.1557130 |
| 22.345 | Conjoint Analysis | User Preference | doi:10.1145/1557019.1557138 |
| 22.075 | Optimization Task | Gradient Descent Algorithm | doi:10.1145/1557019.1557129 |
| 20.349 | Optimization Task | Gradient Descent Algorithm | doi:10.1145/1557019.1557100 |
| 21.788 | Set | Pattern | doi:10.1145/1557019.1557071 |
| 19.849 | Set | Pattern | doi:10.1145/1557019.1557077 |
| 21.047 | Training Dataset | Performance Measure | doi:10.1145/1557019.1557144 |

**Table 4 – A sample of candidate relations (and their source document) with high likelihood score predicted by SDOI as candidates for addition to the kddo1 ontology. The table groups candidates that refer to the same concept pairs.**

However, we performed a bootstrap experiment by iteratively selecting the 10% of relation mentions that were predicted to be True with the highest likelihood score, and then labelled these candidates as True in the subsequent iteration (even if no

[5] We used SVMlight's real-number predictions, and did not boost the selection based on whether more than two documents resulted in predictions for the concept pair.

[6] This task-based result is likely dependent on the maturity of the ontology.

direct link existed in the ontology for the corresponding concept pair).

F1 performance dropped with each iteration. Some analysis can show that this deterioration in performance is unavoidably built into the process: with each iteration the supervised classifier trained models that were based on the increasingly false assumption that True labelled training data were representative of direct links in the ontology. Ensuing models would begin to predict links that were by definition not in the ontology and would thus be evaluated as false positives.
Thus, we again manually inspected the top 40 predicted relations for the first two iterations. The precision dropped after each iteration. After the first iteration, 29 (72.5%) candidates were correct, and after the second iteration, 21 (52.5%) candidates were correct. During the manual review, we observed that predictions in subsequent iterations began to include some of the more common False pairings listed in **Error! Reference source not found.**. Bootstrapping of $SDOI_{rml}$ does not improve the precision of the reported predictions, on the kdd09cma1 benchmark task.

**Observations and Conclusion**

We conclude with some observations based on the predictions reported in **Table 4** of the leave-one-out evaluation on the kdd09cma1 corpus The table includes some promising candidates for addition to the ontology. For example, because of this experiment we noted that the obvious missing direct relation between a Computing System and an Algorithm[7]. The table also includes a more nuanced missing direct relation missing in the ontology between Conditional Probability and Marginal Probability[8].

Next, we observe that suggested relation mention candidates whose concept pairs are predicted within more than one document, such as Computing System + Algorithm, may be more indicative that the direct relation is indeed missing from the ontology than when only supported by a single document. However, as counter-evidence, some of the repeated pairs in **Table 4** appear to be listed simply due to their frequent occurrence in the corpus. For example, the candidate relation between the concepts of Set and of Pattern may simply be due to documents (abstracts) that often mention "*sets of patterns*". We would not expect the Set concept to be directly linked to every concept in the ontology that can be grouped into a set. This example however does suggest that Pattern + Set may be a common and important concept in the data mining domain to deserve the addition of a Pattern Set concept into the ontology. We note further that very frequent candidates, such as Research Paper + Algorithm, were not predicted; likely because the algorithm recognized that if such a commonplace relation is always false then it likely will be false in a new/unseen document. Thus, there is some evidence that the number of repetitions can indeed signify a more likely candidate. As future work, it would be worthwhile to attempt to train a second classifier that can use the number of referring documents as a feature.

A separate challenge that we observe from the predictions in **Table 4** is illustrated by the Optimization Task + Gradient Descent Algorithm entry. While this seems like a reasonable candidate for addition at first glance, these two concepts are more likely indirectly related via the Optimization Algorithm concept (*an* optimization task *can be solved by an* optimization algorithm; *a* grandient descent algorithm *is an* optimization algorithm.). The resolution of these situations could require additional background knowledge from the ontology, such as relation types, to inform the classifier that in some situations when the parent is linked to the concept then the child is not directly linked to it.

## References

Eugene Agichtein, and Luis Gravano. (2000). Snowball: Extracting Relations from Large Plain-Text Collections. In: Proceedings of the 5th ACM International Conference on Digital Libraries (DL 2000).

[7] The direct relation can naturally added in both directions "*an* ALGORITHM *can be implemented into a* COMPUTING SYSTEM" and "*a* COMPUTING SYSTEM *can implement an* ALGORITHM."
[8] Based on passage "*...assumption made by existing approaches, that the marginal and conditional probabilities are directly related....*" From 10.1145/1557019.1557130 and due to the fact that the two concept descriptions are briefly described in `kddo1`.

Paul Buitelaar, Philipp Cimiano, Peter Haase, and Michael Sintek. (2009). Towards Linguistically Grounded Ontologies. In: Proceedings of the 6th European Semantic Web Conference (ESWC 2009).

Michael Erdmann, Alexander Maedche, Hans-Peter Schnurr, and Steffen Staab. (2000). From Manual to Semi-automatic Semantic Annotation: About Ontology-Based Text Annotation Tools. In: Proceedings of the COLING 2000 Workshop on Semantic Annotation and Intelligent Content.

David Haussler. (1999). Convolution Kernels on Discrete Structures. Technical Report UCSC-CLR-99-10, University of California at Santa Cruz.

Jing Jiang, and ChengXiang Zhai. (2007). A Systematic Exploration of the Feature Space for Relation Extraction. In: Proceedings of NAACL/HLT Conference (NAACL/HLT 2007).

Gabor Melli. (2010). Concept Mentions within KDD-2009 Abstracts (kdd09cma1) Linked to a KDD Ontology (kddo1). In: Proceedings of the 7th International Conference on Language Resources and Evaluation (LREC 2010).

Gabor Melli, and Martin Ester. (2010). Supervised Identification of Concept Mentions and their Linking to an Ontology. In: Proceedings of CIKM 2010.

Gabor Melli, Martin Ester, and Anoop Sarkar. (2007). Recognition of Multi-sentence n-ary Subcellular Localization Mentions in Biomedical Abstracts. In: Proceedings of the 2nd International Symposium on Languages in Biology and Medicine (LBM 2007).

Mike Mintz, Steven Bills, Rion Snow, Dan Jurafsky. (2009). Distant Supervision for Relation Extraction without Labeled Data. In: Proceedings of ACL 2009.

Sebastian Riedel, Limin Yao, and Andrew McCallum. (2010). Modeling Relations and their Mentions without Labeled Text. In: Proceedings of ECML 2010.

Steffen Staab (editor), and Rudi Studer (editor). (2009). Handbook on Ontologies - 2nd Ed. Springer Verlag.

Victoria Uren, Philipp Cimiano, José Iria, Siegfried Handschuh, Maria Vargas-Vera, Enrico Motta, and Fabio Ciravegna. (2006). Semantic Annotation for Knowledge Management: Requirements and a survey of the state of the art. In: Web Semantics: Science, Services and Agents on the World Wide Web, 4(1).

David Yarowsky. (1995). Unsupervised Word Sense Disambiguation Rivaling Supervised Methods. In: Proceedings of the 33rd annual meeting on Association for Computational Linguistics (ACL 1995)

# Cause-Effect Relation Learning

**Zornitsa Kozareva**
USC Information Sciences Institute
4676 Admiralty Way
Marina del Rey, CA 90292-6695
kozareva@isi.edu

## Abstract

To be able to answer the question *What causes tumors to shrink?*, one would require a large *cause-effect* relation repository. Many efforts have been payed on *is-a* and *part-of* relation leaning, however few have focused on *cause-effect* learning. This paper describes an automated bootstrapping procedure which can learn and produce with minimal effort a *cause-effect* term repository. To filter out the erroneously extracted information, we incorporate graph-based methods. To evaluate the performance of the acquired *cause-effect* terms, we conduct three evaluations: (1) human-based, (2) comparison with existing knowledge bases and (3) application driven (SemEval-1 Task 4) in which the goal is to identify the relation between pairs of nominals. The results show that the extractions at rank 1500 are 89% accurate, they comprise 61% from the terms used in the SemEval-1 Task 4 dataset and can be used in the future to produce additional training examples for the same task.

## 1 Introduction

Over the years, researchers have successfully shown how to build ground facts (Etzioni et al., 2005), semantic lexicons (Thelen and Riloff, 2002), encyclopedic knowledge (Suchanek et al., 2007), and concept lists (Katz et al., 2003). Among the most well developed repositories are those focusing on *is-a* (Hearst, 1992) and *part-of* (Girju et al., 2003; Pennacchiotti and Pantel, 2006) relations. However, to be able to answer the question "*What causes tumors to shrink?*", one requires knowledge about *cause-effect* relation.

Other applications that can benefit from *cause-effect* knowledge are the relational search engines which have to retrieve all terms relevant to a query like: "*find all X such that X causes wrinkles*" (Cafarella et al., 2006). Unfortunately to date, there is no universal repository of cause-effect relations that can be used or consulted. However, one would still like to dispose of an automated procedure that can accurately and quickly acquire the terms expressing this relation.

Multiple algorithms have been created to learn relations. Some like TextRunner (Etzioni et al., 2005) rely on labeled data, which is used to train a sequence-labeling graphical model (CRF) and then the system uses the model to extract terms and relations from unlabeled texts. Although very accurate, such methods require labeled data which is difficult, expensive and time consuming to create. Other more simplistic methods that rely on lexico-syntactic patterns (Hearst, 1992; Riloff and Jones, 1999; Pasca, 2004) have shown to be equally successful at learning relations, temporal verb order (Chklovski and Pantel, 2004) and entailment (Zanzotto et al., 2006). Therefore, in this paper, we have incorporated an automated bootstrapping procedure, which given a pattern representing the relation of interest can quickly and easily learn the terms associated with the relation. In our case, the pattern captures the *cause-effect* relation. After extraction, we apply graph-based metrics to rerank the information and filter out the erroneous terms.

The contributions of the paper are:

- an automated procedure, which can learn terms expressing *cause-effect* relation.
- an exhaustive human-based evaluation.
- a comparison of the extracted knowledge with the terms available in the SemEval-1 Task 4 dataset for interpreting the relation between pairs of nominals.

The rest of the paper is organized as follows. The next section describes the term extraction procedure. Section 3 and 4 describe the extracted data and its characteristics. Section 5 focuses on the evaluation and finally we conclude in Section 6.

## 2 Cause-Effect Relation Learning

### 2.1 Problem Formulation

The objectives of cause-effect relation learning are similar to those of any general open domain relation extraction problem (Etzioni et al., 2005; Pennacchiotti and Pantel, 2006). The task is formulated as:

> **Task**: Given a *cause-effect* semantic relation expressed through lexico-syntactic pattern and a seed example for which the relation is true, the objective is to learn from large unstructured amount of texts terms associated with the relation.

For instance, given the relation *cause* and the term *virus* for which we know that it can cause something, we express the statement in a recursive pattern[1] "* *and virus cause* *" and use the pattern to learn new terms that cause or have been caused by something. Following our example, the recursive pattern learns from the Web on the left side terms like {*bacteria, worms, germs*} and on the right side terms like {*diseases, damage, contamination*}.

### 2.2 Knowledge Extraction Procedure

For our study, we have used the general Web-based class instance and relation extraction framework introduced by (Kozareva et al., 2008; Hovy et al., 2009). The procedure is minimally supervised and achieves high accuracy of the produced extractions.

**Term Extraction:** To initiate the learning process, the user must provide as input a seed term $Y$ and a recursive pattern *"X* and Y verb Z*"* from which terms on the $X^*$ and $Z^*$ positions can be learned. The input pattern is submitted to Yahoo!Boss API as a web query and all snippets matching the query are retrieved, part-of-speech tagged and used for term extraction. Only the previously unexplored terms found on $X^*$ position are used as seeds in the subsequent iteration, while the rest of the terms[2] are kept. The knowledge extraction terminates when there are no new extractions.

**Term Ranking:** Despite the specific lexico-syntactic construction of the pattern, erroneous extractions are still produced. To filter out the information, we incorporate the harvested terms on $X^*$ and $Y^*$ positions in a directed graph $G$=$(V, E)$, where each vertex $v \in V$ is a candidate term and each edge $(u, v) \in E$ indicates that the term $v$ is generated by the term $u$. An edge has weight $w$ corresponding to the number of times the term pair $(u, v)$ is extracted from different snippets. A node $u$ is ranked by $u$=$(\sum_{\forall(u,v)\in E} w(u,v) + \sum_{\forall(v,u)\in E} w(v,u))$ which represents the weighted sum of the outgoing and incoming edges to a node. The confidence in a correct argument $u$ increases when the term discovers and is discovered by many different terms. Similarly, the terms found on $Z^*$ position are ranked by the total number of incoming edges from the $XY$ pairs $z$= $\sum_{\forall(xy,z)\in E'} w(xy, z)$. We assume that in a large corpus as the Web, a correct term $Z^*$ would be frequently discovered by various $XY$ term pairs.

## 3 Data Collection

To learn the terms associated with a cause-effect relation, the user can use as input any verb expressing causality[3]. In our experiment, we used the verb $cause$ and the pattern "* and <seed> cause *", which was instantiated with the seed term $virus$. We submitted the pattern to Yahoo!Boss API as a search query and collected all snippets returned during bootstrapping. The snippets were cleaned from the html tags and part-of-speech tagged (Schmid, 1994). All nouns (proper names) found on the left and right hand side of the pattern were extracted and kept as potential candidate terms of the cause-effect relation.

Table 1 shows the total number of terms found for the $cause$ pattern on $X^*$ and $Z^*$ positions in 19 bootstrapping iterations. In the same table, we also show some examples of the obtained extractions.

| Term Position | #Extractions | Examples |
|---|---|---|
| **X** cause | 12790 | pressure, stress, fire, cholesterol, wars, ice, food, cocaine, injuries bacteria |
| cause **Z** | 52744 | death, pain, diabetes, heart disease, damage, determination, nosebleeds chain reaction |

Table 1: *Extracted Terms.*

[1]A recursive pattern is a lexico-syntactic pattern for which one of the terms is given as input and the other one is an open slot, allowing the learned terms to replace the initial term directly.

[2]Including the terms found on $Z^*$ position.

[3]The user can use any pattern from the thesauri of http://demo.patrickpantel.com/demos/lexsem/thesaurus.htm

## 4 Characteristic of Learning Terms

An interesting characteristic of the bootstrapping process is the speed of leaning, which can be measured in terms of the number of unique terms acquired on each bootstrapping iteration. Figure 1 shows the bootstrapping process for the *"cause"* relation. The term extraction starts of very slowly and as bootstrapping progresses a rapid growth is observed until a saturation point is reached. This point shows that the intensity with which new elements are discovered is lower and practically the bootstrapping process can be terminated once the amount of newly discovered information does not exceed a certain threshold. For instance, instead of running the algorithm until complete exhaustion (19 iterations), the user can terminate it on the 12th iteration.

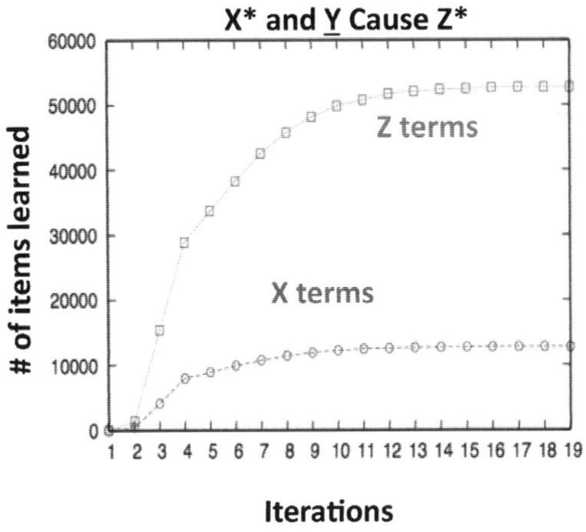


Figure 1: Learning Curve.

The speed of leaning depends on the way the $X$ and $Y$ terms relate to each other in the lexico-syntactic pattern. For instance, the more densely connected the graph is, the shorter (i.e., fewer iterations) it will take to acquire all terms.

## 5 Evaluation and Results

In this section, we evaluate the results of the term extraction procedure. To the extend to which it is possible, we conduct a human-based evaluation, we compare results to knowledge bases that have been extracted in a similar way (i.e., through pattern application over unstructured text) and we show how the extracted knowledge can be used by NLP applications such as relation identification between nominals.

### 5.1 Human-Based Evaluation

For the human based evaluation, we use two annotators to judge the correctness of the extracted terms. We estimate the correctness of the produced extractions by measuring *Accuracy* as the number of *correctly* tagged examples divided by the total number of examples.

Figure 2, shows the accuracy of the bootstrapping algorithm with graph re-ranking in blue and without graph re-ranking in red. The figure shows that graph re-ranking is effective and can separate out the erroneous extractions. The overall extractions produced by the algorithm are very precise, at rank 1500 the accuracy is 89%.

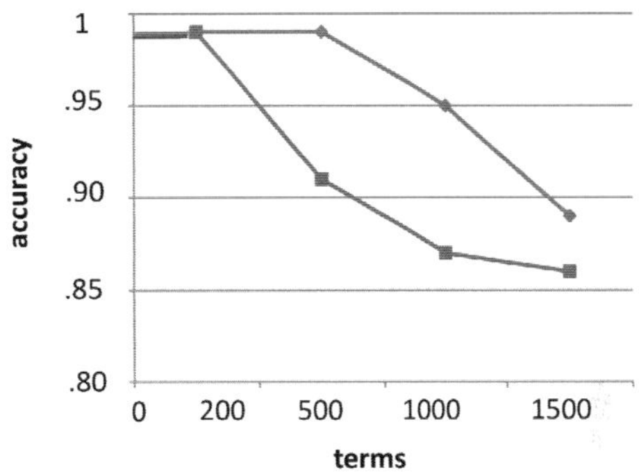


Figure 2: Term Extraction Accuracy.

Next, in Table 2, we also show a detailed evaluation of the extracted $X$ and $Z$ terms. We define five types according to which the humans can classify the extracted terms. The types are: *PhysicalObject*, *NonPhysicalObject*, *Event*, *State* and *Other*. We used *Other* to indicate erroneous extractions or terms which do not belong to any of the previous four types. The Kappa agreement for the produced annotations is 0.80.

| **X** Cause | A1 | A2 | Cause **Z** | A1 | A2 |
|---|---|---|---|---|---|
| PhysicalObj | 82 | 75 | PhysicalObj | 15 | 20 |
| NonPhysicalObj | 69 | 66 | NonPhysicalObj | 89 | 91 |
| Event | 21 | 24 | Event | 72 | 72 |
| State | 29 | 31 | State | 50 | 50 |
| Other | 3 | 4 | Other | 5 | 4 |
| Acc. | .99 | .98 | Acc. | .98 | .98 |

Table 2: *Term Classification.*

### 5.2 Comparison against Existing Resources

To compare the performance of our approach with knowledge bases that have been extracted in a similar way (i.e., through pattern application over unstructured text), we consult the freely available resources NELL (Carlson et al., 2009), Yago

(Suchanek et al., 2007) and TextRunner (Etzioni et al., 2005). Although these bases contain millions of facts, it turns out that NELL and Yago do not have information for the cause-effect relation. While the online demo of TextRunner has query limitation, which returns only the top 1000 snippets. Since we do not have the complete and ranked output of TextRunner, comparing results in terms of relative recall and precision is impossible and unfair. Therefore, we decided to conduct an application driven evaluation and see whether the extracted knowledge can aid an NLP system.

### 5.3 Application: Identifying Semantic Relations Between Nominals

**Task Description** (Girju et al., 2007) introduced the SemEval-1 Task 4 on the Classification of Semantic Relations between Nominals. It consists in given a sentence: *"People in Hawaii might be feeling <e1>aftershocks</e1> from that powerful <e2>earthquake</e2> for weeks."*, an NLP system should identify that the relationship between the nominals *earthquake* and *aftershocks* is *cause-effect*.

**Data Set** (Girju et al., 2007) created a dataset for seven different semantic relations, one of which is *cause-effect*. For each relation, the nominals were manually selected. This resulted in the creation of 140 training and 80 testing cause-effect examples. From the train examples 52.14% were positive (i.e. correct cause-effect relation) and from the test examples 51.25% were positive.

**Evaluation and Results** The objective of our application driven study is to measure the overlap of the cause-effect terms learned by our algorithm and those used by the humans for the creation of the SemEval-1 Task4 dataset. There are 314 unique terms in the train and test dataset for which the *cause-effect* relation must be identified. Out of them 190 were also found by our algorithm.

The 61% overlap shows that either our cause-effect extraction procedure can be used to automatically identify the relationship of the nominals or it can be incorporated as an additional feature by a more robust system that relies on semantic and syntactic information. In the future, the extracted knowledge can be also used to create additional training examples for the machine learning systems working with this dataset.

Table 3 shows some of the overlapping terms in our system and the (Girju et al., 2007) dataset.

| |
|---|
| tremor, depression, anxiety, surgery, exposure, sore throat, fulfillment, yoga, frustration, inhibition, inflammation, fear, exhaustion, happiness, growth, evacuation, earthquake, blockage, zinc, vapour, sleep deprivation, revenue increase, quake |

Table 3: *Overlapping Terms.*

## 6 Conclusion

We have described a simple web based procedure for learning cause-effect semantic relation. We have shown that graph algorithms can successfully re-rank and filter out the erroneous information. We have conduced three evaluations using human annotators, comparing knowledge against existing repositories and showing how the extracted knowledge can be used for the identification of relations between pairs of nominals.

The success of the described framework opens up many challenging directions. We plan to expand the extraction procedure with more lexico-syntactic patterns that express the *cause-effect* relation[4] such as *trigger*, *lead to*, *result* among others and thus enrich the recall of the existing repository. We also want to develop an algorithm for extracting cause-effect terms from non contiguous positions like *"stress is another very important cause of diabetes"*. We are also interested in studying how the extracted knowledge can aid a commonsense causal reasoner (Gordon et al., 2011; Gordon et al., 2012) in understanding that if a girl wants to wear earrings it is more likely for her to get her ears pierced rather then get a tattoo. This example is taken from the Choice of Plausible Alternatives (COPA) dataset[5], which presents a series of forced-choice questions such that each question provides a premise and two viable cause or effect scenarios. The goal is to choose a correct answer that is the most plausible cause or effect. Similarly, the cause-effect repository can be used to support a variety of applications, including textual entailment, information extraction and question answering

## Acknowledgments

We would like to thank the reviewers for their comments and suggestions. The research was supported by DARPA contract number FA8750-09-C-3705.

[4]These patterns can be acquired from an existing paraphrase system.

[5]http://people.ict.usc.edu/ gordon/copa.html

## References

Michael Cafarella, Michele Banko, and Oren Etzioni. 2006. Relational Web Search. In *World Wide Web Conference, WWW 2006*.

Andrew Carlson, Justin Betteridge, Estevam R. Hruschka Jr., and Tom M. Mitchell. 2009. Coupling semi-supervised learning of categories and relations. In *Proceedings of the NAACL HLT 2009 Workskop on Semi-supervised Learning for Natural Language Processing*.

Timothy Chklovski and Patrick Pantel. 2004. Verbocean: Mining the web for fine-grained semantic verb relations. In *Proceedings of EMNLP 2004*, pages 33–40.

Oren Etzioni, Michael Cafarella, Doug Downey, Ana-Maria Popescu, Tal Shaked, Stephen Soderland, Daniel S. Weld, and Alexander Yates. 2005. Unsupervised named-entity extraction from the web: an experimental study. *Artificial Intelligence*, 165(1):91–134, June.

Roxana Girju, Adriana Badulescu, and Dan Moldovan. 2003. Learning semantic constraints for the automatic discovery of part-whole relations. In *Proc. of the 2003 Conference of the North American Chapter of the Association for Computational Linguistics on Human Language Technology*, pages 1–8.

Roxana Girju, Preslav Nakov, Vivi Nastaste, Stan Szpakowicz, Peter Turney, and Deniz Yuret. 2007. SemEval-2007 task 04: Classification of semantic relations between nominals. In *SemEval 2007*.

Andrew Gordon, Cosmin Bejan, and Kenji Sagae. 2011. Commonsense causal reasoning using millions of personal stories. In *Proceedings of the Twenty-Fifth Conference on Artificial Intelligence (AAAI-11)*.

Andrew Gordon, Zornitsa Kozareva, and Melissa Roemmele. 2012. Semeval-2012 task 7: Choice of plausible alternatives: An evaluation of commonsense causal reasoning. In *Proceedings of the 6th International Workshop on Semantic Evaluation (SemEval 2012)*.

Marti Hearst. 1992. Automatic acquisition of hyponyms from large text corpora. In *Proc. of the 14th conference on Computational linguistics*, pages 539–545.

Eduard Hovy, Zornitsa Kozareva, and Ellen Riloff. 2009. Toward completeness in concept extraction and classification. In *Proceedings of the 2009 Conference on Empirical Methods in Natural Language Processing*, pages 948–957.

Boris Katz, Jimmy Lin, Daniel Loreto, Wesley Hildebrandt, Matthew Bilotti, Sue Felshin, Aaron Fernandes, Gregory Marton, and Federico Mora. 2003. Integrating web-based and corpus-based techniques for question answering. In *Proceedings of the twelfth text retrieval conference (TREC)*, pages 426–435.

Zornitsa Kozareva, Ellen Riloff, and Eduard Hovy. 2008. Semantic class learning from the web with hyponym pattern linkage graphs. In *Proceedings of ACL-08: HLT*, pages 1048–1056.

Marius Pasca. 2004. Acquisition of categorized named entities for web search. In *Proc. of the thirteenth ACM international conference on Information and knowledge management*, pages 137–145.

Marco Pennacchiotti and Patrick Pantel. 2006. Ontologizing semantic relations. In *ACL-44: Proceedings of the 21st International Conference on Computational Linguistics and the 44th annual meeting of the Association for Computational Linguistics*, pages 793–800.

Ellen Riloff and Rosie Jones. 1999. Learning dictionaries for information extraction by multi-level bootstrapping. In *AAAI '99/IAAI '99: Proceedings of the Sixteenth National Conference on Artificial intelligence*.

Helmut Schmid. 1994. Probabilistic part-of-speech tagging using decision trees.

Fabian M. Suchanek, Gjergji Kasneci, and Gerhard Weikum. 2007. Yago: a core of semantic knowledge. In *WWW '07: Proceedings of the 16th international conference on World Wide Web*, pages 697–706.

Michael Thelen and Ellen Riloff. 2002. A Bootstrapping Method for Learning Semantic Lexicons Using Extraction Pattern Contexts. In *Proc. of the 2002 Conference on Empirical Methods in Natural Language Processing*, pages 214–221.

Fabio Massimo Zanzotto, Marco Pennacchiotti, and Maria Teresa Pazienza. 2006. Discovering asymmetric entailment relations between verbs using selectional preferences. In *Proceedings of the 21st International Conference on Computational Linguistics and 44th Annual Meeting of the Association for Computational Linguistics*, pages 849–856.

# Bringing the Associative Ability to Social Tag Recommendation

**Miao Fan,**★◇ **Yingnan Xiao**◇ and **Qiang Zhou**★
★ Department of Computer Science and Technology, Tsinghua University
◇School of Software Engineering, Beijing University of Posts and Telecommunications
{fanmiao.cslt.thu,lxyxynt}@gmail.com,
zq-lxd@mail.tsinghua.edu.cn

## Abstract

Social tagging systems, which allow users to freely annotate online resources with tags, become popular in the Web 2.0 era. In order to ease the annotation process, research on social tag recommendation has drawn much attention in recent years. Modeling the social tagging behavior could better reflect the nature of this issue and improve the result of recommendation. In this paper, we proposed a novel approach for bringing the associative ability to model the social tagging behavior and then to enhance the performance of automatic tag recommendation. To simulate human tagging process, our approach ranks the candidate tags on a weighted digraph built by the semantic relationships among meaningful words in the summary and the corresponding tags for a given resource. The semantic relationships are learnt via a word alignment model in statistical machine translation on large datasets. Experiments on real world datasets demonstrate that our method is effective, robust and language-independent compared with the state-of-the-art methods.

## 1 Introduction

Social tagging systems, like Flickr[1], Last.fm[2], Delicious[3] and Douban[4], have recently become major infrastructures on the Web, as they allow users to freely annotate online resources with personal tags and share them with others. Because of the no vocabulary restrictions, there are different kinds of tags, such as tags like keywords, category names or even named entities. However, we can still find the inner relationship between the tags and the resource that they describe. Figure 1 shows a snapshot of a social tagging example, where the famous artist, Michael Jackson was annotated with multiple social tags by users in Last.fm[2]. Actually, Figure 1 can be divided into three parts, which are *the title*, *the summary* and *the tags* respectively.

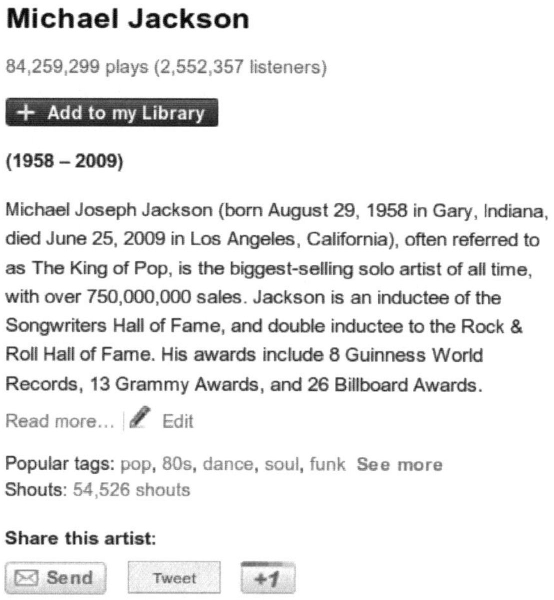


Figure 1: A music artist entry from website Last.fm[2]

We can easily find out that social tags concisely indicate the main content of the given online resource and some of them even reflect user interests. For this reason, social tagging has been widely studied and applied in recommender systems (Eck et al., 2007; Musto et al., 2009; Zhou et al., 2010), advertising (Mirizzi et al., 2010), etc.

For the sake of easing the process of user annotation and providing a better effect of human-computer interaction, researchers expected to build

[1] http://www.flickr.com
[2] http://www.lastfm.com
[3] http://delicious.com
[4] http://www.douban.com

automatic social tagging recommender systems, which could automatically suggest proper tags for a user when he/she wants to annotate an online resource. By observing huge amount of online resources, researchers found out that most of them contain summaries, which could play an important role in briefly introducing the corresponding resources, such as the artist entry about Michael Jackson in Figure 1. Thus some of them proposed to automatically suggest tags based on resource summaries, which are collectively known as the *content-based approach* (F. Ricci et al., 2011).

The basic idea of *content-based approach* in recommender systems is to select important words from summaries as tags. However, this is far from adequate as not all tags are statistically significant in the summaries. Some of them even do not appear in the corresponding summaries. For example, in Figure 1, the popular tag *dance* does not appear in the summary, but why most of users choose it as a proper tag to describe Michael Jackson. This "out-of-summary" phenomenon reflects a fact that users usually exploit their own knowledge and associative ability to annotate online resources. When a summary comes, they associate the important words in the summary with other semantic-related tags based on their knowledge. To improve the automatic tag recommendation, a social computing issue (Wang et al., 2007), modeling the *social tagging behavior* is the straightforward way. Namely, how to analyze the human tagging process and propose a suitable approach that can help the computer to simulate the process are what we will explore in this paper.

The novel idea of our approach is to rank the candidate tags on a weighted digraph built by the semantic relationships among meaningful words in the summary and the corresponding tags for a given resource. The semantic relationships are learnt via a word alignment model in statistical machine translation. Our approach could bring the associative ability to social tag recommendation and naturally simulate the whole process of human social tagging behavior and then to enhance the performance of automatic tag recommendation. So, we name this approach for *Associative Tag Recommendation* (ATR).

The remainder of the paper is organized as follows. Section 2 analyzes the process of human tagging behavior. Section 3 describes our novel approach to simulate the process of human tagging behavior for social tag recommendation. Section 4 compares our approach with the state-of-the-art and baseline methods and analyzes the parameter influences. Section 5 surveys some related work in social tag recommendation. Section 6 concludes with our major contributions and proposes some open problems for future work.

## 2 Human Tagging Behavior Analysis

Here, we will analyze the human tagging process to discover the secret why some of the tags are widely annotated while are not statistically significant or even do not appear in the summaries.

In most cases, the information in summaries is too deficient for users to tag resources or to reflect personalities. Users thus exploit their own knowledge, which may be partly learnt from other resource entries containing both summaries and tags in Table 1. Then when they want to tag an online resource, they will freely associate meaningful words in the summary with other semantic related words learnt from former reading experiences. However, the result of this association behavior will be explosive. Users should judge and weigh these candidate tags in brain, usually via forming a semantic related word network and finally decide the tags that they choose to annotate the given resource.

For example, after browsing plentiful of summary-tag pairs, we could naturally acquire the semantic relationships between the words, such as "singer", "pop", in the summary and the tag, "dance". If we tag the artist entry in Figure 1, the tag "dance" is more likely associated by the words like "pop", "artist", "Rock & Roll" et al. While reading the summary of artist Michael Jackson in Figure 1, we may construct an abstract tag-network in Figure 2 with the important words (king, pop, artist et al.) in the summary, the associated tags (dance, 80s, pop et al) and their semantic relationships.

| |
|---|
| **Summary:** David Lindgren (born April 28, 1982 in Skelleftea, Sweden) is a Swedish ***singer*** and musical artist... |
| **Tags:** swedish, pop, ***dance***, musical, david lindgren |
| **Summary:** Wanessa Godói Camargo (born on |

| |
|---|
| December 28, 1982), known simply as Wanessa, is a Brazilian ***pop singer***... |
| **Tags:** pop, ***dance***, female vocalists, electronic, electropop ... |

Table 1: Examples of artist entries from Last.fm[2]

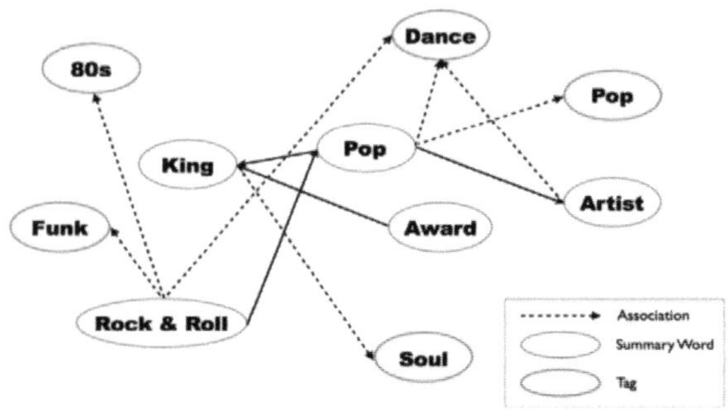


Figure 2: A part of the abstract associative tag-network in human brains.

## 3 Associative Tag Recommendation

We describe our ATR approach as a three-stage procedure by simulating the human annotation process analyzed in Section 2. Figure 3 shows the overall structure of our approach.

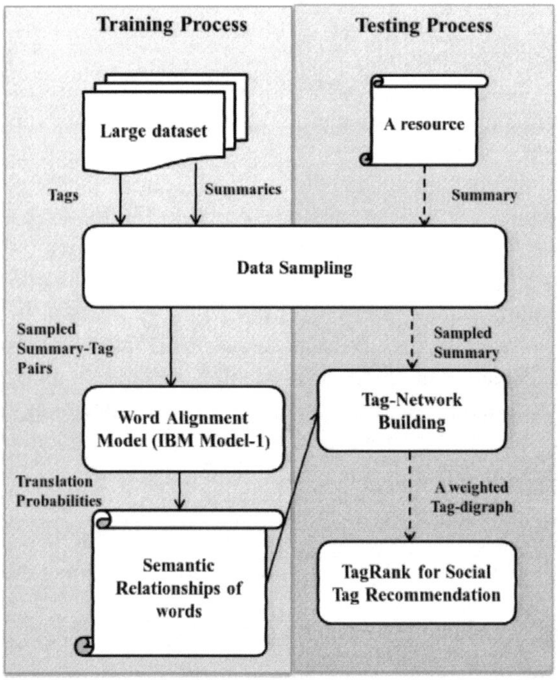


Figure 3: The overview of ATR approach.

**Stage 1: Summary-tag pairs sampling.** Given a large collection of tagged resources, we need to pre-process the dataset. Generally, the pre-processing contains tokenizing the summaries, extracting the meaningful words and balancing the length ratio between the summaries and tags.

**Stage 2: Associative ability acquiring.** We regard a summary-tag pair as a parallel text. They are really suitable to acquire the semantic relation knowledge by using word alignment model (In this paper, we adopt IBM Model-1) from the large amount of summary-tag pairs prepared by Stage 1. After gaining the translation probabilities between the meaningful words in summaries and tags, our social tagging recommender system initially has the capability of association, namely from one word to many semantic related tags.

**Stage 3: TagRank algorithm for recommendation.** Stage 2 just helps our recommender system acquire the ability of associating one word with many semantic related tags. However, when the system faces a given resource with a long summary, the association results may be massive. Thus, we propose a TagRank algorithm to order the candidate tags on the weighted Tag-digraph, which is built by the meaningful words in the summary and their semantic related words.

Before introducing the approach in details, we define some general notations, while the other specific ones will be introduced in the corresponding stage. In our approach, a resource is denoted as $r \in R$, where $R$ is the set of all resources. Each resource contains a summary and a set of tags. The summary $s_r$ of resource is simply regarded as a bag of meaningful words $w_r = \{(w_i, cw_i)\}_{i=1}^{N_r}$, where $cw_i$ is the count of meaningful word $w_i$ and $N_r$ is the number of the unique meaningful words in $r$. The tag set (annotations) $a_r$ of resource $r$ is represented as $a_r = \{(t_i, ct_i)\}_{i=1}^{M_r}$, where $ct_i$ is the count of tag $t_i$ and $M_r$ is the number of the unique tags for $r$.

### 3.1 Summary-Tag Pairs Sampling

We consider that the *nouns* and *tags* that appear in the corresponding summary are *meaningful* for our tagging recommendation approach.

It is not difficult for language, such as English, French et al. As for Chinese, Thai and Japanese, we still need to do word segmentation (D. D. Palmer., 2010). Here, to improve the segmentation results of these language texts, we collect all the unique tags in resource $r$ as the user dictionary to solve the out-of-vocabulary issue. This idea is inspired by M. Sun (2011) and we will discuss its effort on the performance improvement of our system in Section 4.3.

After the meaningful words have been extracted from the summaries, we regard the summary and the set of tags as two bags of the sampled words without position information for a given resource. The IBM Model-1(Brown et al., 1993) was adopted for training to gain the translation probabilities between the meaningful words in summary and the tags. Och and Ney (2003) proposed that the performance of word alignment models would suffer great loss if the length of sentence pairs in the parallel training data set is unbalanced. Moreover, some popular online resources may be annotated by hundreds of people with thousands of tags while the corresponding summaries may limit to hundreds of words. So, it is necessary to propose a sampling method for balanced length of summary-tag pairs.

One intuitional way is to assign each meaningful word in summaries and tags with a term-frequency (TF) weight, namely $cw_i$ and $ct_i$. For each extracted meaningful word $w_i$ in a given summary $s_r$, $TF_{w_i}^{s_r} = \frac{cw_i}{\sum_{i=1}^{N_r} cw_i}$ and the same tag set (annotations) $a_r$, $TF_{t_i}^{a_r} = \frac{ct_i}{\sum_{i=1}^{M_r} ct_i}$. Here, we bring a parameter δ in this stage, which denotes the length ratio between the sampled summary and tag set, namely, $\delta = N_r / M_r$

## 3.2 Associative Ability Acquiring

IBM Model-1 could help our social tagging recommender system to learn the lexical translation probability between the meaningful words in summaries and tags based on the dataset provided by stage 1. We adjust the model to our approach, which can be concisely described as,

$$\Pr(W_r \mid T_r) = \sum_A \Pr(W_r, A | T_r) \quad (1)$$

For each resource $r$, the relationship between the sampled summary $W_r = \{w_i\}_{i=1}^{N_r}$ and the sampled tags $T_r = \{t_i\}_{i=1}^{M_r}$ is connected via a hidden variable $A = \{a_i\}_{i=1}^{N_r}$. For example, $a_j = i$ indicates word $w_j$ in W at position $j$ is aligned to tag $t_i$ in T at position $i$.

For more detail description on mathematics, the joint likelihood of $W_r$ and an alignment $A$ given $T_r$ is

$$\Pr(W_r, A | T_r) = \frac{\varepsilon}{(M_r + 1)^{N_r}} \prod_{j=1}^{N_r} p(w_j \mid t_{a_j}) \quad (2)$$

in which $\varepsilon \equiv \Pr(N_r \mid T_r)$ and $p(w_j \mid t_{a_j})$ is called the translation probability of $w_j$ given $t_{a_j}$. The alignment is determined by specifying the values of $a_j$ for j from 1 to $N_r$, each of which can take any value from 0 to $M_r$. Therefore,

$$\Pr(W_r | T_r) = \frac{\varepsilon}{(M_r + 1)^{N_r}} \sum_{a_1=0}^{M_r} \cdots \sum_{a_{N_r}=0}^{M_r} \prod_{j=1}^{N_r} p(w_j \mid t_{a_j}) \quad (3)$$

The goal is to adjust the translation probabilities so as to maximize $\Pr(W_r | T_r)$ subject to the constraints that for each t,

$$\sum_w p(w|t) = 1 \quad (4)$$

IBM Model-1 can be trained using Expectation-Maximization (EM) algorithm (Dempster et al., 1977) in an unsupervised fashion. At last, we obtain the translation probabilities between summaries and tags, i.e., $p(w|t)$ and $p(t|w)$ for our recommender system acquiring associative ability.

From Eq. (4), we know that IBM Model-1 will produce one-to-many alignments from one language to another language, and the trained model is thus asymmetric. Sometimes, there are a few translation pairs appear in both two direction, i.e., summary → tag ($p_{s2t}$) and tag → summary ($p_{t2s}$). For this reason, Liu et al. (2011) proposed a harmonic means to combine the two models.

$$p(t|w) = \left(\frac{\lambda}{p_{t2s}(t|w)} + \frac{1-\lambda}{p_{s2t}(t|w)}\right)^{-1} \quad (5)$$

### 3.3 TagRank Algorithm for Recommendation

By the time we have generated the "harmonic" translation probability list between meaningful words in summaries and tags, our recommender system could acquire the capability of association like human beings. For instance, it could "trigger" a large amount of semantic related tags from a given word: *Novel* (Figure 4). However, if we collected all the "triggered" tags associated by each meaningful word in a given summary, the scale would be explosive. Thus we need to explore an efficient way that can not only rank these candidate tags but also simulate the human tagging behavior as much as possible.

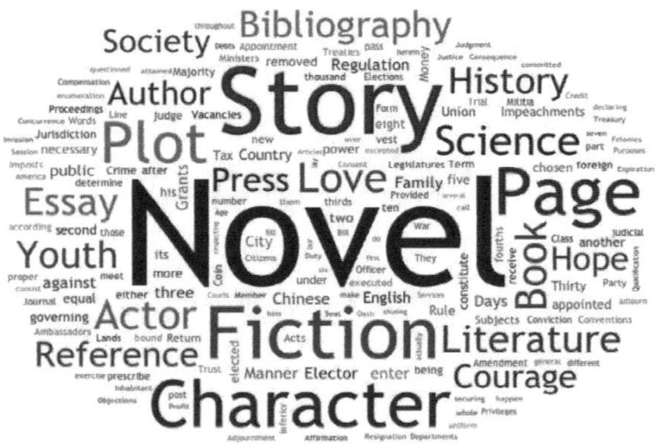


Figure 4: The association results from the word "Novel" via our social tagging recommender system.

Inspired by the PageRank algorithm (S. Brin and L. Page., 1998), we find out that the idea could be brought into our approach with a certain degree improvement as the human tagging ranking process is on a weighted Tag-digraph G. We regard the association relationship as one word recommending the corresponding candidate tags and the degree of preference could be quantified by the translation probabilities.

For a given summary, we firstly sample it via the method described in stage 1 to obtain all the meaningful words, which are added to the graph as a set of seed vertices denoted as $V_s$. Then according to stage 2, we could obtain a set of semantic related vertices associated by these seeds denoted as $V_a$. We union the $V_a$ and $V_s$ to get the set of all candidate tags $V$. For a directed edge $e_{ij}$ from $v_i$ to $v_j$, the weight $w(e_{ij})$ equals the translation probability from $v_i$ to $v_j$, namely $p(v_j|v_i)$. So the weighted Tag-digraph could be formulized as,

$$\begin{cases} G = (V, E) \\ V = V_s \cup V_a \\ E = \{e_{ij}\} \\ e_{ij} = \{(v_i, v_j), v_i, v_j \in V\} \\ w(e_{ij}) = p(v_j|v_i) \end{cases} \quad (6)$$

The original TextRank algorithm (Mihalcea et al., 2004) just considered the words recommending the nearest ones, and assumed that the recommending strengths were same. As all the words had the equal chance to recommend, it was the fact that all the edges in the graph gained no direction information. So this method brought little improvement on ranking results. In the Eq. (7) they used, $In(v_i)$ represents the set of all the vertices that direct to $v_i$ and $Out(v_j)$ denotes the set of all the vertices that direct from $v_j$. The factor $d$ is usually set to 0.85.

$$\text{Score}(v_i) = (1-d) + d * \sum_{v_j \in In(v_i)} \frac{1}{|Out(v_j)|} \text{Score}(v_j) \quad (7)$$

We improve the TextRank model and propose a TagRank algorithm (Eq. 8) that is suitable to our approach. For each $v_j$, $\frac{w(e_{ji})}{\sum_{v_k \in Out(v_j)} w(e_{jk})}$ represents the proportion of trigger ability from $v_j$ to $v_i$. This proportion multiplying the own score of $v_j$ reflect the the degree of recommend contribution to $v_i$. After we sum up all the vertices willing to "recommend" $v_i$, namely $v_j \in In(v_i)$, We can calculate the score of $v_i$ in one step.

Some conceptual words could trigger hundreds of tags, so that our recommender system will suffer a rather high computation complexity. Thus, we add a parameter θ which stands for the maximum out-degree of the graph G. That means for each vertex in the graph G, it can at most trigger top-θ candidate tags with the θ highest translation probabilities.

$$\mathrm{Score}(v_i) = (1-d) + d * \sum_{v_j \in In(v_i)} \frac{\mathrm{w}(\mathrm{e}_{ji})}{\sum_{v_k \in Out(v_j)} \mathrm{w}(\mathrm{e}_{jk})} \mathrm{Score}(v_j) \quad (8)$$

Starting from *vertex initial values* assigned to the seed nodes ($V_s$) in the graph, the computation iterates until convergence below a given threshold is achieved. After running the algorithm, a score is assigned to each vertex. Finally, our system can recommend best M tags with high score for the resource.

# 4 Experiments

## 4.1 Datasets and Evaluation Metrics

**Datasets:** We prepare two real world datasets with diverse properties to test the performance of our system in different language environment. Table 2 lists the statistical information of the English and Chinese datasets.

| Dataset | $P$ | $V_s$ | $V_t$ | $N_s$ | $N_t$ |
|---|---|---|---|---|---|
| BOOK | 29464 | 68996 | 40401 | 31.5 | 7.8 |
| ARTIST | 14000 | 35972 | 4775 | 19.0 | 5.0 |

Table 2: Statistical information of two datasets. $P$, $V_s$, $V_t$, $N_s$, and $N_t$ represent the number of parallel texts, the vocabulary of summaries, the vocabulary of tags, the average number of unique words in each summary and the average number of unique tags in each resource respectively.

The first dataset, BOOK, was crawled from a popular Chinese book review online community Douban[4], which contains the summaries of books and the tags annotated by users. The second dataset, ARTIST, was freely obtained via the Last.fm[2] API. It contains the descriptions of musical artists and the tags annotated by users. By comparing the characteristics of these two datasets, we find out that they differ in language, data size and the length ratio (Figure 5). The reason of preparing two datasets with diverse characteristics is that we would like to demonstrate that our approach is effective, robust and language-independent compared with others.

**Evaluation Metrics:** We use precision, recall and F-measure to evaluate the performance of our ATR approach. Given a resource set $R$, we regard the set of original tags as $T_O$, the automatic recommended tag set as $T_R$. The correctly recommended set of tags can be denoted as $T_R \cap T_O$. Thus, precision, recall and F-measure are defined as[5]

$$p = \frac{|T_R \cap T_O|}{|T_R|}, r = \frac{|T_R \cap T_O|}{|T_O|}, F = \frac{2\,p\,r}{(p+r)} \quad (9)$$

The final precision and recall of each method is computed by performing 7-fold cross validation on both two datasets.

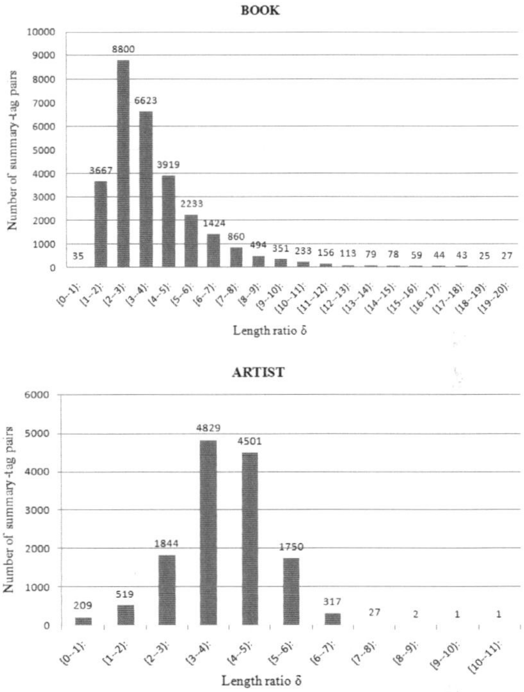


Figure 5: The length ratio distributions of BOOK and ARTIST datasets.

## 4.2 Methods Comparison

**Baseline Methods:** In this section, we compare the performance of our associative tagging recommendation (ATR) with three other relative methods, the state-of-the-art WTM (Liu et al., 2011), TextRank (Mihalcea et al., 2004) and the traditional TFIDF (C. D. Manning et al., 2008; R. Baeza-Yates et al., 2011).

[5] The reason why we do not calculate the precision, recall and F-measure alone is that we cannot guarantee that recommending at least one correct tag for each resource.

The reasons we choose those methods to compare were as follows.

- WTM can reflect the state-of-the-art performance on *content-based* social tag recommendation.
- TextRank can be regarded as a baseline method on graph-based social tag recommendation.
- TFIDF, as a traditional method, represents the baseline performance and can validate the "out-of-summary" phenomenon.

For the TFIDF value of each word in a given summary, it can be calculated by multiplying term frequency $TF_{w_i}^{S_r} = 1 + \log\frac{cw_i}{\sum_{i=1}^{N_r} cw_i}$ (log normalization) by inverted document frequency $IDF_{w_i}^{S_r} = \log(1 + \frac{|R|}{\left|\sum_{r \in R} I_{cw_i > 0}\right|})$ (inverse frequency smooth), where $\left|\sum_{r \in R} I_{cw_i > 0}\right|$ indicates the number of resources whose summaries contain word $w_i$.

TextRank method regarded the word and its forward and backward nearest words as its recommendation. Thus, each word in a given summary is recommended by its neighborhood with no weight. Simply, we use Eq. (7) to calculate the final value of each word in a given summary.

Liu et al. (2011) proposed a state of the art method which summed up the product the weight of a word and its translation probabilities to each semantic related tag as the final value of each tag in a given resource (Eq. 10).

$$\Pr(\mathrm{t}|\mathrm{w}_r) = \sum_{w \in \mathrm{w}_r} \Pr(t|w)\Pr(w|\mathrm{w}_r) \quad (10)$$

**Experiment Results:** Figure 6 illustrates the precision-recall curves of ATR, WTM, TextRank and TFIDF on two datasets. Each point of a precision-recall curve stands for different number of recommended tags from M = 1 (upper left) to M = 10 (bottom right). From the Figure 6, we can observe that:

- ATR out-performs WTM, TextRank and TFIDF on both datasets. This indicates that ATR is a language-independent approach for social tag recommendation.
- ATR shows consistently better performance when recommending different number of tags, which implies that our approach is efficient and robust (Figure 7).

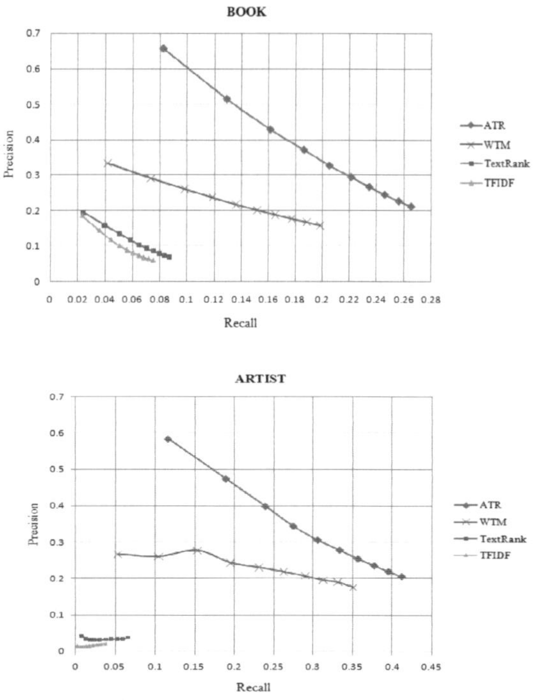


Figure 6: Performance comparison among ATR, WTM, TextRank and TFIDF on BOOK and ARTIST datasets when $\lambda = 0.5$ , $\theta = 5$ and vertex initial values are assigned to one.

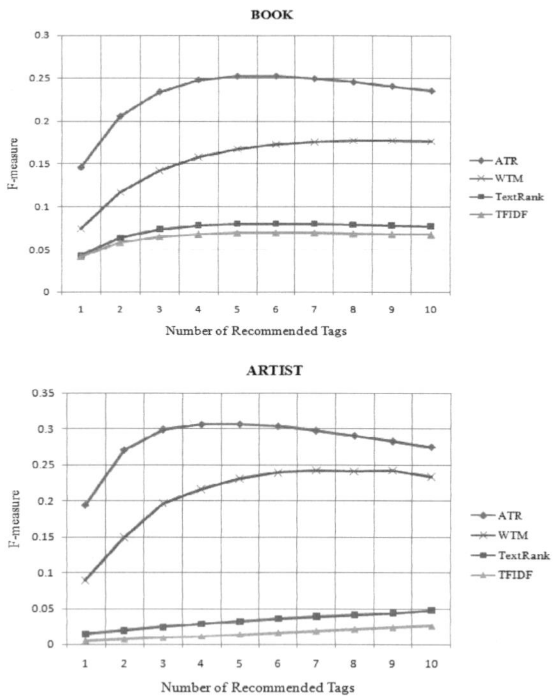

Figure 7: F-measure of ATR, WTM, TextRank and TFIDF versus the number of recommended tags (M) on the BOOK and ARTIST datasets when $\lambda = 0.5, \theta = 5$ and vertex initial values are assigned to one.

### 4.3 Sampling Methods Discussion

Section 3.1 proposed an idea on summary-tag pairs sampling, which collected all the unique tags as the user dictionary to enhance performance of the summary segmentation, especially for the Chinese, Thai, and Japanese et al. Though M. Sun (2011) put forward a more general paradigm, few studies have verified his proposal. Here, we will discuss the efficiency of our sampling method. Figure 8 shows the comparison of performance between the unsampled ATR and (sampled) ATR.

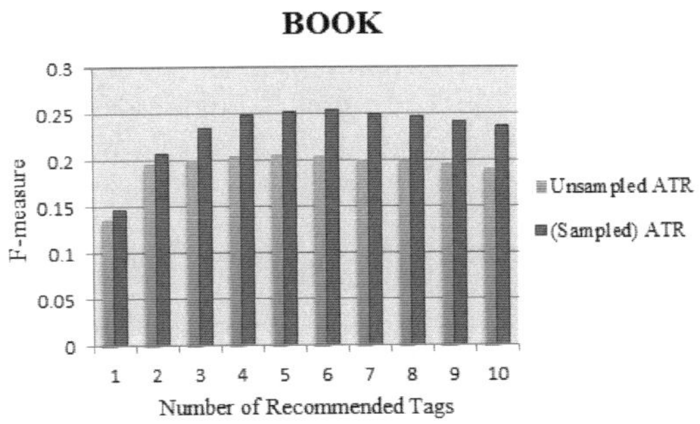


Figure 8: Performance comparison between unsampled ATR and (sampled) ATR on BOOK datasets when $\lambda = 0.5, \theta = 5$ and vertex initial values are assigned to one

Experiments on the Chinese dataset BOOK demonstrates that our (sampled) ATR approach achieves average 19.2% improvement on performance compared with the unsampled ATR.

### 4.4 Parameter Analysis

In Section 3, we brought several parameters into our approach, namely the harmonic factor $\lambda$which controls the proportion between model $p_{t2s}$ and $p_{s2t}$, the maximum out-degree $\theta$ which specifies the computation complexity of the weighted tag-digraph and the vertex initial values which may affect the final score of some vertices if the weighted tag-digraph is not connected.

We take the BOOK dataset as an example and explore their influences to ATR by using controlling variables method, which means we adjust the focused parameter with the other ones stable to observe the results.

**Harmonic factor:** In Figure 9, we investigate the influence of harmonic factor via the curves of F-measure of ATR versus the number of recommended tags on the BOOK dataset. Experiments showed that the performance is slightly better when $\lambda = 0.0$. As $\lambda$ controls the proportion between model $p_{t2s}$ and $p_{s2t}$, $\lambda = 0.0$ means model $p_{t2s}$ contributes more on performance.

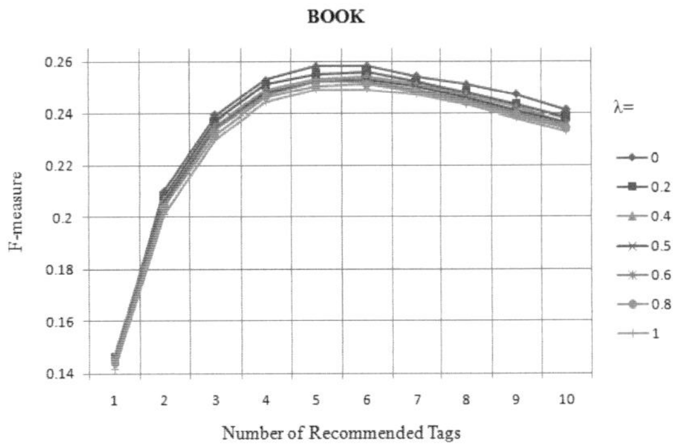


Figure 9: F-measure of ATR versus the number of recommended tags on the BOOK dataset when harmonic factor $\lambda$ ranges from 0.0 to 1.0, when $\theta = 5$ and vertex initial values are assigned to one.

**Maximum out-degree:** Actually, during the experiments, we have found out that some meaningful words could trigger hundreds of candidate tags. If we bring all these tags to our Tag-Network, the computation complexity will be dramatically increased, especially in large datasets. To decrease the computation complexity with little impact on performance, we need to explore the suitable maximum out-degree. Figure 10 illustrates how the complexities of tag-digraph will influent the performance. We discover that ATR gains slight improvement when $\theta$ is added from 5 to 9 except the "leap" from 1 to 5. It means that $\theta = 5$ will be a suitable maximum out-degree, which balances the performance and the computation complexity.

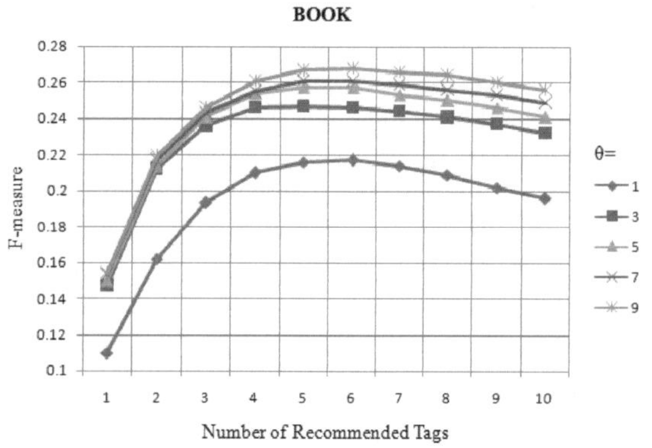


Figure 10: F-measure of ATR versus the number of recommended tags on the BOOK dataset, when $1 \leq \theta \leq 9, \lambda = 0.2$ and vertex initial values are assigned to one.

**Vertex initial values:** The seeds (meaningful words in the summaries) may not be semantic related, especially when the maximum out-degree is low. As a result, the graph G may be disconnected, so that the final score of each vertex after iteration may relate to the vertex initial values. In Figure 11, we compare three different vertex initial values, namely value-one, value of TF (local consideration) and value of TFIDF (global consideration) to check the influence. However, the results show that there is almost no difference in F-measure when the maximum out-degree θ ranges from 1 to 9.

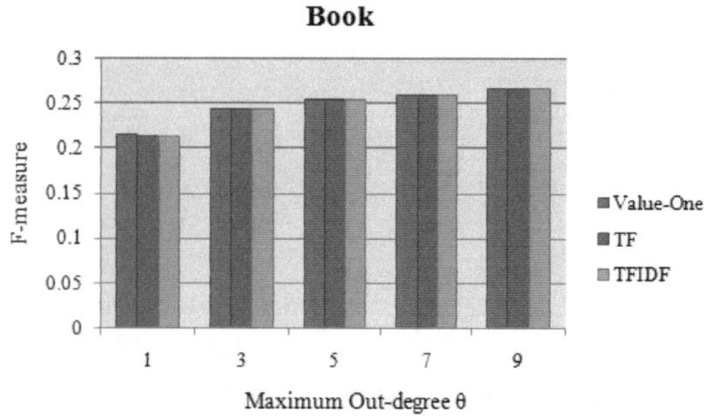


Figure 11: F-measure of ATR versus maximum out-degree on BOOK dataset when the vertex initial values equal to Value-One, TF, TFIDF separately with $\lambda = 0.2$ and number of recommended tags M = 5.

## 5 Related Work

There are two main stream methods to build a social tag recommender system. They are collaboration-based method (Herlocker et al., 2004) and the content-based approach (Cantador et al., 2010).

FolkRank (Jaschke et at., 2008) and Matrix Factorization (Rendle et al., 2009) are representative collaboration-based methods for social tag recommendation. Suggestions of these techniques are based on the tagging history of the given resource and user, without considering the resource summaries. Thus most of these methods suffer from the cold-start problem, which means they cannot perform effective suggestions for resources that no one has annotated.

To remedy the defect of cold-start problem, researchers proposed content-based methods exploiting the descriptive information on resources, such as summaries. Some of them considered social tag recommendation as a classification problem by regarding each tag as a category label. Various classifiers such as kNN (Fujimura et al., 2007), SVM (Cao et al., 2009) have been discussed. But two issues exposed from these methods.

- Classification-based methods are highly constrained in the quality of annotation, which are usually noisy.
- The training and classification cost are often in proportion to the number of classification labels, so that these methods may not be efficient for real-world social tagging system, where thousands of unique tags may belong to a resource.

With the widespread of latent topic models, researchers began to pay close attention on modeling tags using Latent Dirichlet Allocation (LDA) (Blei et al., 2003). Recent studies (Krestel et al., 2009; Si and Sun, 2009) assume that both tags and words in summary are generated from the same set of latent topics. However, most latent topic models have to pre-specify the number of topic before training. Even though we can use cross validation to determine the optimal number of topics (Blei et al., 2010), the solution is obviously computationally complicated.

The state of the art research on social tagging recommendation (Z. Liu, X. Chen and M. Sun, 2011) regarded social tagging recommendation problem as a task of selecting appropriate tags from a controlled tag vocabulary for the given resource and bridged the vocabulary gap between the summaries and tags using word alignment models in statistical machine translation. But they simply adopted the weighted sum of the score of candidate tags, named word trigger method (WTM), which cannot reflect the whole process of human annotation.

## 6 Conclusion and Future Work

In this paper, we propose a new approach for social tagging recommendation via analyzing and modeling human associative annotation behaviors. Experiments demonstrate that our approach is effective, robust and language-independent compared with the state of the art and baseline methods.

The major contributions of our work are as follows.

- The essential process of human tagging process is discovered as the guideline to help us build simulating models.
- A suitable model is proposed to assist our social tagging recommender system to learn the semantic relationship between the meaningful words in summaries and corresponding tags.
- Based on the semantic relationship between the meaningful words in the summaries and corresponding tags, a weighted Tag-digraph is constructed. Then a TagRank algorithm is proposed to re-organize and rank the tags.

Our new approach is also suitable in the tasks of keyword extraction, query expansion et al, where the human associative behavior exists. Thus, we list several open problems that we will explore in the future:

- Our approach can be expanded from lexical level to sentence level to bring the associative ability into semantic-related sentences extraction.
- We will explore the effects on other research areas, such as keyword extraction, query expansion, where human associative behavior exists as well.

## Acknowledgements

The work was supported by the research projects of National Science Foundation of China (Grant No. 60873173) and National 863 High-Tech research projects (Grant No. 2007AA01Z173). The authors would like to thank Yi Luo for his insightful suggestions.

## References

R. Baeza-Yates and B. Ribeiro-Neto. 2011. *Modern information retrieval: the concepts and technology behind search, 2nd edition*. ACM Press.

D. M. Blei, A. Y. Ng, and M. I. Jordan. 2003. Latent dirichlet allocation. JMLR, 3:993-1022.

S. Brin and L. Page. 1998. The anatomy of a large-scale hypertextual web search engine. *Computer networks and ISDN systems*, 30 (1-7): 107-117.

P. F. Brown, V. J. D. Pietra, S. A. D. Pietra, and R. L. Mercer. 1993. The mathematics of statistical machine translation: Parameter estimation. *Computational linguistics*, 19(2):263-311.

I. Cantador, A. Bellogín, D. Vallet. 2010. Content-based recommendation in social tagging systems. *In Proceedings of ACM RecSys*, pages 237-240.

H. Cao, M. Xie, L. Xue, C. Liu, F. Teng, and Y. Huang. 2009. Social tag predication base on supervised ranking model. *In Proceeding of ECML/PKDD 2009 Discovery Challenge Workshop*, pages 35-48.

A. P. Dempster, N. M. Laird, D. B. Rubin, et al. 1977. Maximum likelihood from incomplete data via the em algorithm. *Journal of the Royal Statistical Society*. Series B (Methodological), 39 (1): 1-38.

D. Eck, P. Lamere, T. Bertin-Mahieux, and S. Green. 2007. Automatic generation of social tags for music recommendation. *In Proceedings of NIPS*, pages 385-392.

S. Fujimura, KO Fujimura, and H. Okuda. 2007. Blogosonomy: Autotagging any text using bloggers' knowledge. *In Proceedings of WI*, pages 205-212.

J. L. Herlocker, J. A. Konstan, L. G. Terveen, and J. T. Riedl. 2004. Evaluating collaborative filtering recommender systems. *ACM Transactions on Information Systems*, 22(1):5-53.

R. Jaschke, L. Marinho, A. hotho, L. Schmidt-Thieme, and G. Stumme. 2008. Tag recommendations in social bookmarking systems. *AI Communications*, 21(4):231-247.

R. Krestel, P. Fankharser, and W. Nejdl. 2009. Latent dirichlet allocation for tag recommendation. *In Proceedings of ACM RecSys*, pages 61-68.

Z. Liu, X. Chen, M. Sun. 2011. A simple word trigger method for social tag suggestion. *In Proceedings of EMNLP*, pages 1577-1588.

C. D. Manning. P. Raghavan, and H. Schtze. 2008. *Introduction to information retrieval*. Cambridge University Press, NY, USA.

R. Mihalcea and P. Tarau. 2004. TextRank: Bringing order into texts. *In Proceedings of EMNLP*, pages 404-411. Poster.

R. Mirizzi, A. Ragone, T. Di Noia, and E. Di Sciascio. 2010. Semantic tags generation and retrieval for online advertising. *In Proceedings of CIKM*, pages 1089-1098.

C. Musto, F. Narducci, M. de Gemmis, P. Lops, and G. Semeraro. 2009. STaR: a social tag recommender system. *In Proceeding of ECML/PKDD 2009 Discovery Challenge Workshop*, pages 215-227.

F. J. Och and H. Ney. 2003. A systematic comparison of various statistical alignment models. *Computational linguistics*, 29(1): 19-51.

D. D. Palmer. 2010. Text preprocessing. *Handbook of natural language processing 2nd edition*, chapter 2. CRC Press.

S. Rendle, L. Balby Marinho, A. Nanopoulos, and L. Schmidt-Thieme. 2009. Learning optimal ranking with ensor factorization for tag recommendation. *In Proceedings of KDD*, pages 727-726.

F. Ricci, L. Rokach, B. Shapira and P. B. Kantor. 2011. *Recommender Systems Handbook*. Springer Press.

X. Si and M. Sun. 2009. Tag-LDA for scalable real-time tag recommendation. *Journal of Computational Information Systems*, 6(1): 23-31.

M. Sun. 2011. Natural language processing based on naturally annotated web resources. *Journal of Chinese Information Processing*, 25(6): 26-32

T. C. Zhou, H. Ma, M. R. Lyu, and I. King. 2010. UserRec: A user recommendation approach in social tagging systems. *In Proceedings of AAAI*, pages 1486-1491.

# Author Index